Nina Campbell's
Decorating Not book

Nina Campbell's
Decorating Notebook

Insider Secrets and Decorating Ideas
for Your Home

Text by
Alexandra Campbell
Photography by Jan Baldwin

CICO BOOKS
LONDON NEW YORK

I would like to thank my wonderful clients, all of whom have been an inspiration and a pleasure to work

with; all the multi-talented artists, craftsmen, tradesmen, antique dealers and shop owners

with whom I have dealt over many years; and my family, friends and associates

who put up with me being late and overtired on many occasions, due to the stresses

of being an interior designer.

In particular, I would like to thank Jan Baldwin, Cindy Richards,

Marie-Louise Fiske, Alexandra Campbell, Mary Armour, all the team at CICO Books,

John Carter Flowers and Harper & Tom's Flowers.

First published in 2004 by CICO Books
This paperback edition published in 2010 by CICO Books
an imprint of Ryland, Peters & Small
20–21 Jockey's Fields, London WC1R 4BW

WWW.CICOBOOKS.COM

A CIP catalogue record for this book is available from the British Library.

Paperback ISBN-13: 978 1 907030 18 5
(Hardback ISBN-13: 978 1 903116 93 7)

Printed in China

Edited by Alison Wormleighton
Additional styling by Sue Rowlands
Designed by David Fordham

CONTENTS

NINA~ MY STYLE

In my own home I wanted to create a cross between contemporary and classic style. Crisp modern design and antiques can complement each other beautifully, and mixing the two creates a home full of personality. I've always believed in working favourite pieces into new schemes and here I've juxtaposed a David Linley dining table with a set of six Hepplewhite chairs, and contemporary halogen lighting with antique French wall lights.

However, the essential first step is to start with the way you use space and how you want to live. Now that two of my children have left home and the youngest is grown-up, it's not so much a family home as a haven for me, a place to entertain and somewhere that my youngest daughter, while living with me, can enjoy her own independent space.

LEFT: *A mix of contemporary and classic in my drawing room: full-length windows, elaborately dressed, are combined with a 1930s brass-and-silver fire surround, a painting by Sophie Coryndon from the Lucy B. Gallery, and modern architectural touches.*

12

My Master Plan

T his apartment was a lateral conversion – I bought two side-by-side apartments and opened them into one, which resulted in a much more spacious living area. (One was actually a two-storey apartment, so there is some upstairs space, too.) Although you must check building regulations before buying adjacent properties, it's not usually difficult to get planning permission.

If you are planning any major revamping of space, I'd strongly advise working with an architect – in fact, I worked with two. I originally bought the apartment from the architect Roland Cowan and I loved what he'd done with it so much that I asked him to work with me on opening it up. The other was Clive Butcher, who designed such elements as the radiator grilles, bookcases and mirrored architraves.

*How to combine contemporary
and classic style*

ABOVE LEFT: *The picture is from William
Yeoward and the rug from The Rug Company.*
ABOVE: *We created new, outsized doorways
and Clive Butcher framed them with mirrored
architraves.*

LEFT: *Reuse your favourite things. I remember the French bergère chairs in tapestry in my childhood. My mother upholstered them in apricot silk and then I redid them with old curtains. Now this bold stripe is perfect for them. The divided mirror is from Gordon Watson, and the antique wall lights have come with me from house to house.*

Conservation can mean…

LEFT: *My grandmother's antique silver teapot looks glorious in the ultra-modern setting of a stool from Roger Muirhead at Jamb and a pared-down contemporary fireplace. As a child I always loved duck-egg blue rooms with yellow curtains, and these walls in Quench the Gloom from the Paint Library are the updated version.*

MAKING THE SPACE WORK

I don't believe in changing things for the sake of it, and this apartment already had a smart stainless steel contemporary galley kitchen and conservatory-style eating area just off the dining hall. So, although I opened up the dining hall to the drawing room on either side of the fireplace, I left the kitchen almost untouched. Instead, I concentrated my efforts on revolutionizing other aspects, such as the entrances and doorways. Two apartments mean two front doors, so we gained living space by getting rid of one and removing its corridor. As for storage, we tucked cupboards and bookcases into every possible corner, cutting them into lots of different sizes and shapes to get them in. We even lined the internal staircase up to where my daughter and guests sleep on the second floor with bookcases.

Although I like a stripped-back style, I feel that it's important to respect period detail. It's always worth finding out how to replace this sort of detail properly – for example, what the depth of the skirting boards (baseboards) should be for the date of the house.

…keeping it modern

18

ABOVE AND RIGHT: *Use decorative detail or small amounts of modern fabric to update tradition. I used a modern Galbraith & Paul fabric on the Hepplewhite chairs, and glass beading to edge the cream damask curtains. Grand curtain treatments work when the windows are the right proportions.*

I have a passion
for decorating tables

21

LEFT AND ABOVE: *Combine antique china with cheaper items. I buy it from a wide variety of sources, ranging from expensive antique shops to eBay. I collect items like this apple-green milk glass, and enjoy ferreting about in my china cupboard to mix rather than match.*

LEFT AND RIGHT: *Mirror glass in furniture is fashionable, but be careful – using lots of pieces of reflective glass together can distort images unless done expertly. Be sure to commission it from someone who knows what they are doing.*

This is the dining room in its 'hall' mode, with books and flowers. I always think that a dining room needs to be part of the flow of a home. Take a room like this: if it is closed off, it becomes a room for entertaining only.

The beautiful mirrored cabinet, which I commissioned from William Yeoward, serves as my china cupboard. I didn't want either a painted cabinet or a solid wood one, so we came up with this pattern of mirror glass which reflects light into the room, looks modern and yet is not overbearing. By breaking up the glass into small rectangles, you're not faced with blank sheets. The bottom consists of radiator covers.

The pattern on the chairs draws the whole room together. A room without any pattern may look modern but it will also often look bland.

Try simple contrasts of blue and white for a classic modern look

24

ABOVE LEFT: *A close-up of the chair covers made of linen from Croatia.*
ABOVE: *The glass is from Annabel Elliot Ltd.*
RIGHT: *You don't always have to hang mirrors singly – grouping two or more together is a lovely way of using light as a decorative feature.*

THIS IS HOW I USE WHITE

The eating area, which has huge windows overlooking a small roof terrace, is light and bright, so I painted it white. Blue and white is a classic combination, but it always looks fresh and modern too. This space is long and narrow — the stainless steel kitchen is at the other end — and is our everyday eating area. With this and the dining hall, I have enormous flexibility and can entertain any number of guests, from two to twenty-eight! The linen-covered chairs with my initial on them have a nice history. I sent linen seeds to Croatia to help them restart their linen business, and they sent me a bolt of the resulting linen in return, which now covers these dining chairs. There wasn't quite enough so we backed them in a check from Nicole Fabre.

LEFT AND THIS PAGE: *Think big in small spaces. If your outside sitting area is small, like mine on the roof terrace, be lavish with generous-sized furniture and accessories.*

27

The small roof terrace juts out onto the street over the front door, and my first priority was to make it safe. Because the floor was already decked, the railings seemed too low to me, so I ringed the whole terrace with tall metal boxes – which were painted the colour of the outside of the house so they didn't look conspicuous from the street – and put in the topiary hedge you can see behind the sofa. I decided to make it a summer sitting area rather than an eating area, because the conservatory table is so close that I knew we'd never need to eat out here. I have furnished it like a room inside, with a huge sofa and comfortable cushions (which stay outside all summer long). It now takes at least six people for drinks in the summer, which is perfect.

Start with comfort and luxury
in a bedroom

RIGHT: *When fitting cupboards or bookcases, think about how they would look if the room changed use. The dressing table, made by Ria Augusti, could double as a desk. An outsize chandelier adds drama – in this position no one is going to bang their head on it. The hydrangea pattern on the curtains is my Hortensia fabric.*

HOW TO PLAN FOR THE FUTURE

My bedroom is where the old front door to the second apartment used to be, and because of the fire regulations, I have had to keep it there, disguised by fabric on the walls and by pictures. I was able to make the room bigger by taking out the corridor, however, and I added a fire surround to an unused fireplace. I don't like seeing blocked-in fireplaces or chimney breasts without a function, so even if you can't use the fireplace, I think it's nice to have one there.

Perhaps one day I will move my bedroom upstairs, and, if so, this little room could become a library, or maybe a library cum second bedroom. I planned it with that in mind, using the same wooden flooring as the rest of the apartment. On the floor is a shaggy rug by Deirdre Dyson. There is a full wall of bookcases on either side of the window, which not only makes the window look attractively deeper but also offers lots of extra storage space.

When planning bookcases, pay attention to detail. Always make sure the shelving is strong enough to hold the books – nothing looks worse than sagging shelves. The sides should be a little thicker than the shelves themselves. I also prefer bookcases to extend all the way to the ceiling and I always have adjustable shelves for flexibility. Here I've added a decorative fillip by painting the insides of the bookcases violet.

BELOW: *Fabric disguises the bedroom's jib door, retained for fire regulations; wrapping it around the door is not a job for amateurs. A high, square-edged headboard adds a modern look.*
BELOW RIGHT: *Use colour to soften the hard lines of a bathroom.*

In my bathroom I wanted a sleek, modern look but not a cold, hard one. I therefore chose a soft colour for the walls – my own lavender paint – and bathroom fittings that combine the flowing lines of traditional shapes with cool, clean, modern design. The free-standing bath is almost, but not quite, like a classic claw-foot bath, and the pedestal basin, too, would have looked appropriate at any time in the last

Free-standing fittings
make the room seem bigger

hundred years. Although it is a small room, I've managed to tuck a wall of full-length cupboards in at the end – never neglect the opportunity to add storage. However, built-in cupboards aren't necessarily the only choice when space is tight. The amount of visible floor space is what is most important: the more floor you can see, the bigger the bathroom will look.

Stow away storage on the stairs

BELOW: *In the stairwell, the bookcases lined with books provide their own abstract pattern.*
RIGHT: *This dramatic painting by Patrice Lombardi creates impact in the dining room.*

32

MAKING AN IMPACT

With its oversized doors, mirrored handles and modern art, the stairwell is contemporary — but the rich amethyst paint colour is also warm and welcoming. Note the clear handrail and the way the bookcases have been set into the stairway. The table is from Nico de Villeneuve.

*Always make the space
work well first*

I Need Flexibility

Upstairs is an apartment within an apartment, which is a good way of living with an adult son or daughter while you both retain your independence. With my grown-up daughter, we could have chosen to have both our bedrooms upstairs, but I felt that this arrangement – a separate bathroom, bedroom and sitting room upstairs for her and my bedroom downstairs off the drawing room – would be better.

The first task, though, was to make the space work well, because the rooms were small and narrow. We took down a wall, creating a nicely shaped 5.5 x 4m (18 x 13ft) sitting room. Don't be afraid of reducing the value of a property by losing a room – if the result looks and works better, you won't.

The sitting room has an extra element, a mini-kitchen area, so that my daughter can make herself toast up here if she wants to. But it is very discreet and could easily be taken out or turned into built-in storage.

As usual, I have reupholstered and reused much of the furniture from my previous home – I strongly believe that people may not want, or may not be able, to start again from scratch, so giving old furniture a new lease of life is at the heart of my philosophy. The curtains, for example, in the top left-hand picture opposite, came from my old apartment, and have been made to fit a slightly larger window by adding a contrasting band of linen.

ABOVE, CLOCKWISE FROM TOP LEFT: *Four quick tips: Add edging to curtains to update them and make them bigger; make radiator covers interesting with carved panels; I prefer high beds and therefore high bedside tables; blinds (shades) take up less space in small rooms.*

1 If you have tall windows, you can afford to make a dramatic flourish. Update the look with a beaded trim and a contrast lining on the tails (cascades).

7 The right fabric can really pull a room together. The colours in this fabric reflect those of the room, and the Galbraith & Paul circle design is fresh and crisp.

6 I like an upholstered back on a sofa — you spend less time plumping up cushions.

5 A multicoloured carpet gives you the opportunity of using a variety of schemes.

2

I bought this little tub chair at an antique fair. It is the model for my own Brewster chair and looks modern while fitting in perfectly with a classic scheme. Always have a variety of different seating in a drawing room.

3

I covered the tub chairs in this beautiful olive mohair, which picks up the colour from the floral painting above the fireplace.

4

My favourite chair has been with me all my life; it is now covered in this smart stripe.

NINA'S NOTEBOOK

KEY DECORATING DECISIONS

● In my own home, I love to combine classic and contemporary, and to ensure a successful mix, I treat cushions, trimming, lampshades and other accessories as the shoes and handbags of the home. The right shoes can really make an outfit — and equally, if you have the wrong shoes, you can feel old-fashioned in the smartest of suits. Give a lot of thought to home accessories, and don't hang onto old lampshades or faded cushions for years after they should have been thrown away.

● Most people want to stick to some kind of budget and so have to make choices about what to spend the money on. Old lampshades and cushions can be the one element that dates a room, so be prepared to change them.

● If you've fallen in love with a dramatic fabric, think about using it as here, on smaller items such as cushions or chairs, where it will be less overwhelming than on sofas or curtains.

● Another advantage of accessories is that they are easy to change. The cushions on the sofa shown opposite, for example, link this room to the dining hall next door because the pattern is the same as that of the dining chairs. If I need to seat more people at the sitting-room end, I can bring the dining chairs in.

FLOORPLAN

1 I DON'T BELIEVE in change for the sake of it, so I haven't touched this contemporary kitchen area.

2 THE CONSERVATORY-STYLE DINING AREA overlooks the terrace. I painted it white but didn't change it structurally.

3 THE FRONT DOOR to the left-hand apartment is unchanged as it has become the door to the new, bigger apartment.

4 THE OTHER FRONT DOOR is now closed and covered with fabric, and is a fire door.

5 I REMOVED the old kitchen and moved the wall between it and the bedroom.

6 I REMOVED this bathroom, so that I could make a bigger bathroom off the bedroom at (7) to recreate the original room.

7 THIS SPACE used to be the stairs, which I removed and turned into an ensuite bathroom.

8 THE BEDROOM. A door through from bedroom to bathroom is one of just three openings between the apartments.

9 THE FORMER sitting room of the right-hand flat, this is now a new enlarged drawing room.

10 THE FIREPLACE WALL now faces both ways, between the two new openings to the dining hall from the drawing room.

11 THE DINING HALL opens onto both the conservatory-eating area and the drawing-room area.

12 I BORROWED SPACE from the new bathroom to create a hall cupboard, circular staircase upstairs and WC.

● In my own home I was lucky enough to buy two adjoining apartments on the same level. However, because the walls were such major structural elements, I was only able to knock through in certain places. If you're doing a project like this, rethink everything – bathrooms, kitchens, staircases, and, of course, storage. Treat the space as a completely blank page – you can't get away with just adding a new doorway.

BEFORE

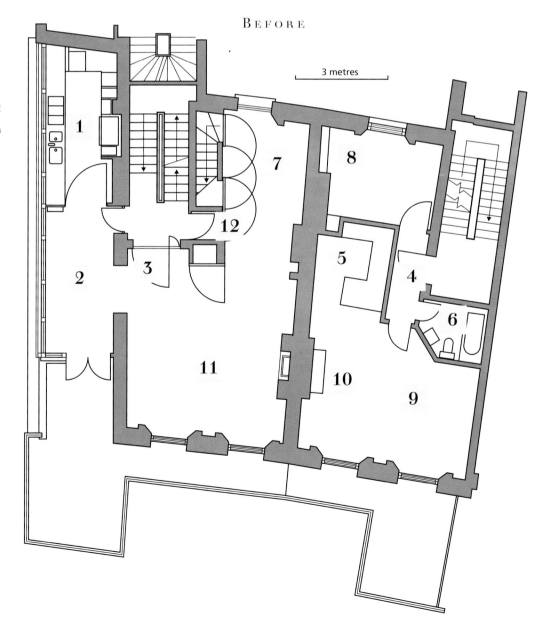

3 metres

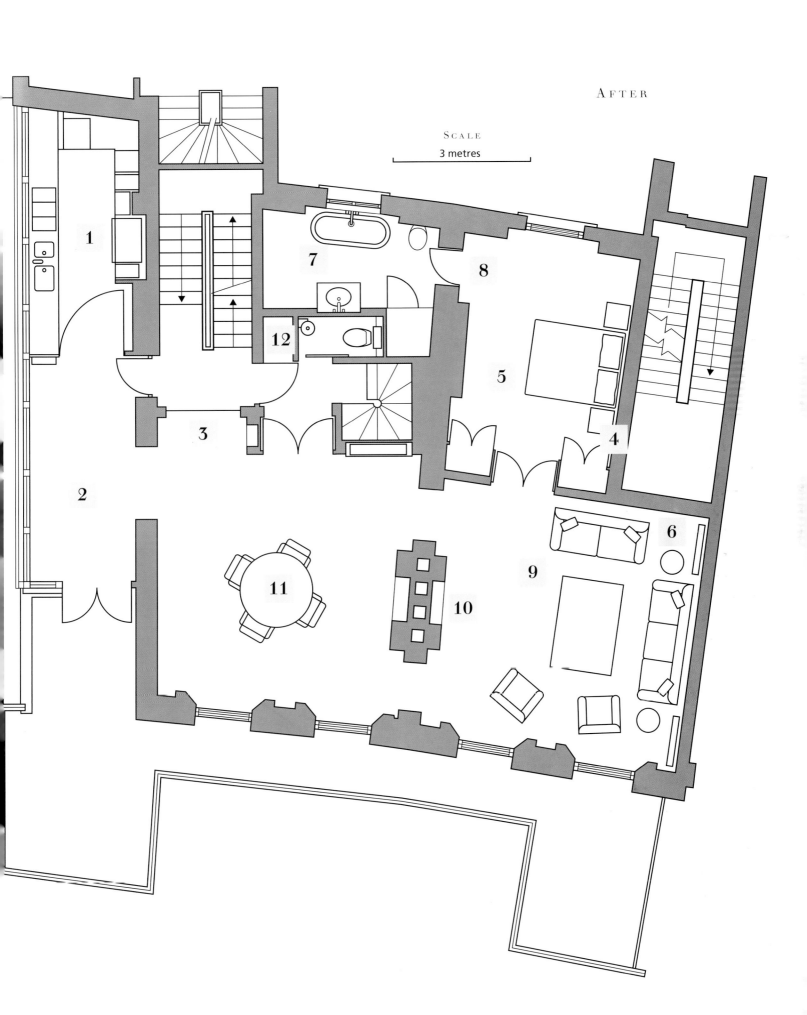

Scale

3 metres

1

7

8

12

5

3

2

4

6

11

10

9

How a House Evolves

I have now got to the stage in my career where some of my original clients are returning to me so that I can update or refurbish my own earlier work. It's not just a question of changing fashion, or furnishings that have begun to look worn, faded or tired – but a family, all families, change continuously over the years. The young couple becomes a family with small children, and the children become teenagers, then grow up and leave home – or, these days, very often don't, but want their own space. This is the case here: I had been asked to come back to redo the dining room, the master bedroom suite and, now that the daughters are grown-up, their adult bedrooms and sitting room.

LEFT: *A formal dining room is a wonderful place to display a collection of silver dishes. The lighting in this room comes from the chandelier (on a dimmer switch, of course), picture lighting, masses of candles and little candle lamps.*

42

If a Colour Works...

The dining room is at the heart of this home because my client is a great hostess and a superb cook. Everyone always wants to come to her dinner parties, and she enjoys giving them. Most of the family meals are taken at home too, so, unlike many dining rooms, this is the hub of the household. The last time we decorated this room, we chose red for the walls, and we decided to stick with it now. I regard red as a 'neutral', and, although my client has a marvellous mix of china and glass, it has all evolved around a red room. I've tweaked the shade a little, however, choosing for the walls my Orleans silk damask, which has a touch of gold in it, instead of the pinky-red we had before. In order to let the magnificently laid table be the star of the show, all the other elements in the room are a harmonious shade of red – the

Updating can mean tweaking, not a major change

43

ABOVE: *Fill different-shaped bowls with different kinds of fruit.*
LEFT: *These gold plates were bought from my shop twenty years ago! The antique side plates don't match – there are six of one set and six of another.*

Red is my favourite for flexibility

curtains are made from the same Orleans silk damask, and the upright dining chairs are in a horizontal velvet stripe from Nobilis. To take advantage of the lovely view from the window in this room, I also added a window seat with a bolster.

When searching for fabric, don't just take 'no' for an answer if you are told that fabric is out of stock. When I was looking for this chair fabric, I was originally told that there was none left, but stock these days is checked by computer, and computers do occasionally get things wrong! This isn't the first time that I've persevered, and in fact when someone went into the warehouse to search, they found that there was fabric left after all.

When you are updating a room, do not simply put pictures back as they were before. Instead, rationalize and rehang them, as I did here – this is worth doing every few years in any house, as things easily get added to and cluttered up.

ABOVE AND RIGHT: *The dining room majors in red, which provides a rich but simple backdrop to glass and china. Attention to detail pays off – note the small studs arranged in a pattern on these dining chairs.*

FAR LEFT AND LEFT: *With furniture reclaimed from elsewhere in the house, the cushions and bookcases helped pull a diverse look together. Low furniture is good in a low room, but the two tall lamps added some contrast of heights.*

MY TIPS FOR ATTIC ROOMS

I was particularly flattered to be asked to do the two daughters' area of the house because daughters often don't want their mother's interior decorator. This room – a sitting room with a kitchen off it – was an attic, with tanks, a place where nobody ever went. Consequently, the living space of the house has increased considerably and the daughters can live quite independently whenever they wish to. As living at home becomes more of a trend, carving an extra sitting room out of dead space in the house can make a great difference.

We decided that a theme reminiscent of a nightclub would be fun. For the furniture, we gathered almost all the pieces – one sofa, two chairs, the rug, the coffee table and the circular shelves by the kitchen – from other areas in the house. Many houses acquire too much furniture over the years, so don't forget that your other rooms may benefit from a clear-out. As this room shows, the result doesn't have to be a ragbag of different styles and colours, so long as you identify one or two colours that are common to, or go with, everything, to pull it all together.

Look at the colours you already have and keep fabrics simple. The theme here is cassis and cream – cream on its own would have been too bland.

Add a warm shade to a neutral

47

Check fire regulations for attic rooms

RIGHT: *The circular shelves were recycled from elsewhere in the house and make a see-through partition between the kitchen and sitting room. Having a kitchen up here as well as a sitting room turns a disused attic into a separate apartment.*

We had one piece of furniture made – a sofa-daybed with a mattress base for unexpected guests. For it, I chose one of my own plain fabrics, Indore Chenille in deep red. With two patterned chairs already in the room, any more pattern would have been too much. The other sofa is cream, like the sloping ceiling. There is already red in the rug and shades of amethyst in the chairs, so it all pulls together with the addition of some cushions, which were chosen to echo colours in the room. This is not the place to add more accent colour or pattern, as the reclaimed furniture is already diverse enough, but by doing it this way we didn't even need to reupholster the chairs. In the kitchen a red Smeg refrigerator continues the colour theme, looking both welcoming and modern – more a work of art than a utilitarian piece.

If you are considering an attic conversion, bear in mind that there are regulations covering access, windows and other aspects, so you will need to consult an architect, structural engineer or attic-conversion specialist. As regards the decoration, you cannot disguise the awkward shapes, limited space, low ceilings and lack of light, so don't try. Instead, make a virtue of necessity. Rather than automatically painting the attic in light shades in an attempt to maximize light that probably isn't there in the first place, think about using intimate, warm colours to create a cosy, welcoming feel.

Light shades suit light rooms

LEFT: *Make storage part of the decor: hats and bags are hung on cupboard door hooks. In the bottom right corner of the photo you can just see a traditional stand for walking sticks, given new life by using it for shoes.*

PRACTICALITY IS MY WATCHWORD

One of today's greatest luxuries is to have a dressing room off the master bedroom, and although the 'dressing room' has traditionally been considered a male domain, it makes much more sense to have one for the mistress of the house. A room like the one pictured here is more than a walk-in wardrobe – as well as wall-to-wall cupboards, it contains a small canopied bed for a midday rest or a restless night, and a couple of comfortable chairs.

This is a lovely, light room so cream was an obvious choice, because when you're dressing you need a fairly calm background for your clothes. We kept all the decoration simple and light for the same reason, but I couldn't resist these hooks on the cupboard doors, on which my client hangs hats and bags. The bags are covered in transparent muslin to protect them, but this way she can enjoy her favourite accessories every day rather than hiding them away in a cupboard.

ABOVE: *Black and white sharpens up a bathroom.*
RIGHT: *Hung on a rail that bows out and up, the curtains match the walls. The pattern is in the undercurtains.*

A QUICK LIFT

The bathroom, which I had decorated fifteen years earlier, didn't need any major restructuring and all the fittings were still good, but my clients wanted it freshened up. The bathroom itself has lots of marble so I decided that black and white would add a crisp, modern look. I found a black settee and covered it with my black-and-white Chinoiserie print. The addition of white linen curtains completed the new look.

The master bedroom in the house, pictured on the right, is a good example of how to use pattern in a bedroom while retaining a calm, serene feel.

THE NEXT STAGE ON

When I decorated my client's daughters' rooms fifteen years ago, they were young children and the result was pink and white chintzy rooms – a heavenly choice for little girls but too saccharine for the sophisticated and talented young women they have become. They are very creative, painting and designing across a wide range of areas, so not only did their bedrooms have to be smart and contemporary, but they had to provide a neutral atmosphere for the art and other items that will be displayed there from time to time. The idea was to simplify the room and make a background for an ever-changing scene.

White, neutral and natural shades offer the best backdrop, but that doesn't mean they have to be uniform and boring. Shades of camel, buff or cream, edged or accented in white or black, can look smart and contemporary and can be mixed with almost any other colour or style. We decided on my Butterscotch paint for the walls, and I edged the cream linen curtains with a wide border of the same fabric – a good way of giving them definition while still remaining in the neutral palette. The black leather sofa came from their father's study and the only bit of permanent colour comes from the striped chenille headboard. The striking red bedspread was made by my client's daughter. Not only does the room look fabulous, but she'll be able to ring the changes as her taste evolves.

Sophisticated and contemporary, but flexible

BELOW AND RIGHT: *Keep fabric colours soft in a cool climate: here my Magnolia fabric picks up on the greens, blues and flowers from the garden, but it also has the requisite delicacy and subtlety that an English garden demands.*

MY GARDEN 'QUICK FIX'

I am not a garden designer, but these days the garden is often an extension of the interior, so my work may take me outside. Once again, I don't believe in buying new furniture for the sake of it, as so many people already have the bones of an excellent layout if only they would look at ways of pulling it together. What I particularly like about this garden is its overgrown, jungly feel. The blue shade of my client's garden furniture works well against the rich greens, so it only remained to choose a fabric for the seat cushions to link it all together.

Fabrics for the garden have got rather stuck in either plain white, cream or deep green canvas or very bright colours and patterns. However, I think that the effect is much better if you look at them in the same way as you do indoor fabrics – think about what is already there and what will go with it.

1 The rich fringing on the curtains matches the silk damask perfectly. If you can't find exactly the colour you want, it may be worth having the trimming custom-made.

6 This beautiful silk damask was used on the walls as well as for the curtains.

NINA'S NOTEBOOK

KEY DECORATING DECISIONS

● When you're trying to decide how to decorate a room, it's always helpful to have a starting point, and while many people may pick a favourite painting or piece of furniture as a kick-off, you could even think about starting with lovely china, particularly if you're revamping a dining room. My client on this project has collected some beautiful china and glass over the years, so I wanted a colour that would act as an equally fabulous backdrop.

● Some people might think that if you're going to all the trouble and expense of decorating, then you will want the new decor to be very different from the existing scheme. This dining room, however, was red previously and is still red today. One reason is that the china and glass particularly suited red, so choosing another colour might have meant buying new china, too. Also, like all walls, curtains and furniture, it has faded and got worn, which is a good enough reason to replace it – but there's no point in changing a good colour scheme just for the sake of it.

● Remember that when it comes to interior design, detail is all-important. This is a lavish, classic red dining room, but it also looks smart and up-to-date because of the little touches, such as the studding on the chairs, the restrained approach to hanging pictures and the use of the latest trimmings and beading on the curtains.

2 Chandeliers look wonderful over dinner tables, but always have them on a dimmer, and experiment with the lighting before guests arrive. I usually suggest dimming them or turning them off, and lighting a dining room with candles and side lamps.

3 Collect candlesticks to make a table welcoming. With shades on candles, don't forget about the fire risk – never leave them unsupervised.

4 The ribbed chenille fabric used on the chairs exactly picks up the colours from the damask. We trimmed them with antique brass studs.

5 You can change the mood of a dining room with different china and glass.

SMALL-SCALE GRANDEUR

There's no need to cramp your style because you live in a small place. When this client downsized her city base from a grand house to a small apartment with low ceilings and no storage space, she still wanted a sense of opulence to set off her wonderful paintings and furniture.

In a small space like this, it's best to keep colours simple. My client wanted red, which delighted me, as it is the perfect background for pictures. It also has a regal magnificence, creating the atmosphere we wanted. As the flat was dark, white would have looked cold and dingy. I chose red and cream, therefore, as the two 'anchor' colours, breaking them up with the richly decorative fabrics and paintings, to create an intimate and elegant feel.

LEFT: *With low ceilings, avoid pendant lighting. The drawing room in this low-ceilinged apartment is lit by lamps; a main dimmer switch changes the lighting from dramatic to cosy in a second. One of the sofas is covered in a floral-printed linen – more modern than chintz – and is positioned away from similar-patterned curtains.*

ABOVE: *'Warm' neutrals like cream and beige look best with red.*
LEFT: *Reflecting lamplight in mirrors is a favourite trick of mine.*

CHANGE DOORS AND OPENINGS

Space planning is always my first priority – here, we opened up the drawing room with double doors from the narrow hallway, creating space to greet guests and draw them through. Although the room had never had a fireplace, I added one to act as a focal point and because it felt appropriate for this style. As the room is dark and is used mainly in the evening, I didn't worry about light, and chose lavish curtains, hung simply. The rails bow outward, making the curtains tie back prettily and adding a curved shape to an angular room, but because of the low ceilings, I've avoided a pelmet.

ABOVE AND RIGHT: *Note how the double doors improve the proportions of this small drawing room. Unity is important in all small spaces – throughout the apartment, the flooring is in the same neutral shade, and these chairs can be used elsewhere when required. A good tip: think about where you are going to position your pictures before you start decorating and furnishing a room.*

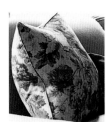

HOW TO USE DEAD SPACE

I am passionate about good room planning, and the small, dark inner hall at the centre of the apartment was our greatest challenge. It had six doors, so I closed off two access doors and turned them into cupboards, providing vital storage. In a small home you have to have a place for everything, because clutter is too noticeable.

I disguised the two cupboard doors by using the same wallpaper as I chose for the walls – my red Veracruz library wallpaper. In addition, I used a richly decorative fabric curtain instead of a door to soften the access from the entrance hallway and save space. With a round table and six chairs, the inner hall became a dining room with the comforting, welcoming feel of a grand library.

Above left: *To vary the red colour theme, the curtain at the doorway to the dining hall introduces several new notes.*
Above: *Red chair fabrics continue the colour theme – avoid having too many contrasts in a small space.*
Right: *This glass cupboard used to be a doorway. As the room it led to is now an en-suite dressing room, the doorway could be used to create a cupboard.*

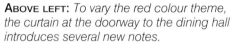

Storage planning is the key

A big picture
looks dramatic in a small room

68

ABOVE AND RIGHT: *Table decorations are a passion of mine. This colour scheme suits the kind of fine china, gilt and porcelain usually seen in a much larger, grander house. My client rings the changes with different tablecloths and alternates flowers with a striking eagle-and-ball centrepiece.*

The magnificent painting pictured here works well in a small space because everything else has been kept simple, if opulent. Just one colour of flooring, a natural beige, is used throughout the apartment. Many people think that small rooms have to have small pictures and furniture, but you can, in fact, create impact and a luxurious effect with one oversized piece.

It's also worth paying attention to detail in small rooms because you will really be able to see it and appreciate it. This apartment originally lacked good architectural detail, so investing in well-made ceiling cornicing, door surrounds and other finishes was important. Not all the doors were disguised with the wallpaper, as this could get confusing – I used a slightly warm white for the two doors leading to actual rooms.

ABOVE AND ABOVE RIGHT: *My toile-de-Jouy wallpaper and fabric are used throughout the bedroom/bathroom/ dressing-room suite. Rather than combining a bright white with red, use a cream tone, for the warmth that red needs. A cool, bright white will look better when blue is your main colour.*

A jewel-box effect in toile de Jouy

HOW TO USE PATTERN

Four-posters and half-testers are not an option for bedrooms in small apartments, but that doesn't mean you can't create an extravagant look. Here I used a combination of thoughtful planning and sumptuous fabric.

This apartment is essentially for one person, plus guests or grandchildren from time to time, so I was able to block off both the main bathroom and the third bedroom to create one bedroom/bathroom/dressing-room suite. As space is tight, the dressing room contains the 'housekeeper's cupboard' – the ironing board, vacuum cleaner and so on. Space was also borrowed from both the bathroom and the dressing room to create cupboards – including one for the washing machine and dryer – on the hall side. I have tucked storage into every possible corner: coats, suitcases, books and hobby paraphernalia must all be considered at the planning stage.

The bathroom is wholly covered, including the ceiling, in my toile-de-Jouy wall-paper, Asticou. This is echoed in the bedroom and dressing room in the curtain, head-board and dressing-table fabric. If you want to use an opulent fabric in a small room, prevent it looking cluttered or fussy by limiting it to just one pattern that you repeat.

1 The textured fabric was used for the curtains and sofa at the other end of the room, and the check for cushions.

2 Use a bowed-out curtain rail to give a soft feel to a room. This treatment, with the curtains meeting at the top, doesn't let in a lot of light, but that's fine for a room mainly used in the evening.

8 If the ceiling is low, a standard lamp can be useful to give a different balance of light because you can't have pendant lights.

7 This beautiful cream flannel covers the sofa, and the fringe helps prevent a line of shoe polish along the bottom.

6 A 'before' picture showing the dining room as it was previously.

3 Don't be afraid to combine printed linens with silk damask.

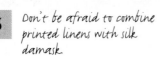

NINA'S NOTEBOOK

4 We covered a pair of bergère chairs in this deep olive damask, which adds contrast to the room.

KEY DECORATING DECISIONS

● This room is like a jewel box – small but rich, and a perfect background for my client's pictures and art. Painting a room a deep colour takes more courage than almost anything, so don't lose your nerve. It is a particularly good way of making small rooms look like something special – as people have known for years when they've painted their studies dark green or their dining rooms red.

● Deep or dark-coloured rooms look good with lots of pictures and ornaments to break up the solid-coloured walls. One reason that the colour here is not too overpowering is that there are so many lovely things to attract the eye, with no vast expanses of colour.

● This is a good demonstration of the reason why white really does not make rooms look either bigger or lighter, as you can see from the little 'before' picture at the bottom of the opposite page. Many people pick white because it seems safe, but I would suggest you only do so when you can prove to yourself that it is the best decorating choice for that room.

5 Olive green and cream make a backdrop that works beautifully with art.

FLOORPLAN

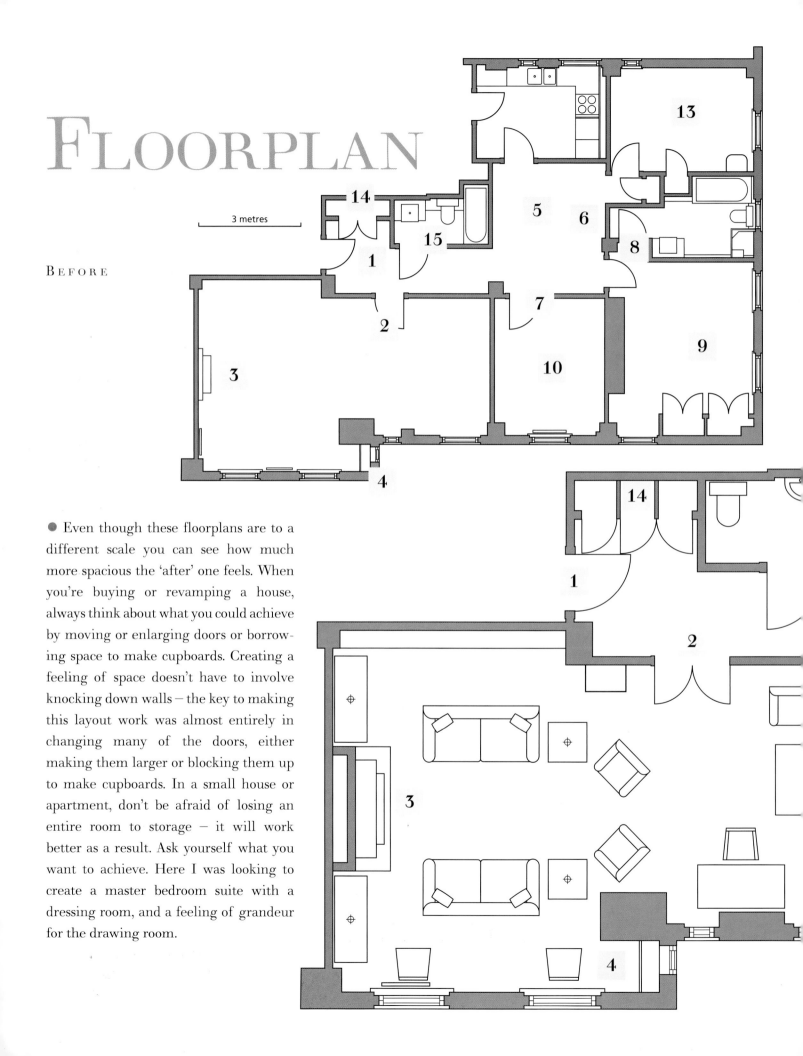

3 metres

BEFORE

● Even though these floorplans are to a different scale you can see how much more spacious the 'after' one feels. When you're buying or revamping a house, always think about what you could achieve by moving or enlarging doors or borrowing space to make cupboards. Creating a feeling of space doesn't have to involve knocking down walls – the key to making this layout work was almost entirely in changing many of the doors, either making them larger or blocking them up to make cupboards. In a small house or apartment, don't be afraid of losing an entire room to storage – it will work better as a result. Ask yourself what you want to achieve. Here I was looking to create a master bedroom suite with a dressing room, and a feeling of grandeur for the drawing room.

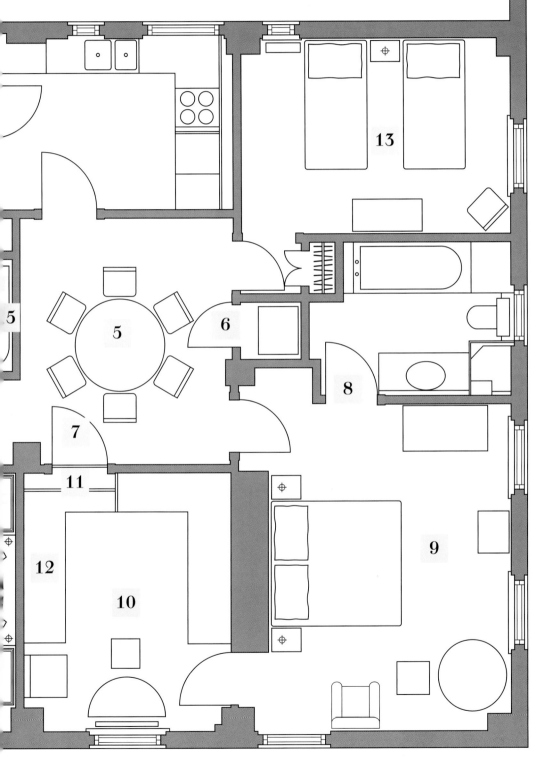

1 THE FRONT DOOR of the apartment opens
onto a narrow corridor with the drawing
room on the right.

2 BY TURNING THIS from a single door into
double doors, I made both drawing room
and hall seem larger.

3 WE CREATED a chimneybreast in this
spot to hold the fireplace and add
depth.

4 THIS ALCOVE HAD a very tiny window.
Now covered over, it offers valuable
storage space.

5 THE CENTRAL DINING HALL has just
enough space for a round table and
six chairs.

6 THIS IS NOW the door to a cupboard
housing the washing machine and
tumble dryer.

7 FORMERLY THE ENTRANCE to bedroom
three, this is now a cupboard housing
glassware (11).

8 I MOVED THE bathroom door to create the
washing-machine cupboard.

9 THE MASTER BEDROOM is still the same
size as before but it now has a second door
leading off.

10 THE DRESSING ROOM contains clothes,
housekeeping necessities and other items,
stored in cupboards (12).

11 THE GLASSWARE CUPBOARD is now
accessed from the dining hall.

12 THE MAIN CUPBOARDS provide storage for
clothes and other items.

13 THE GUEST ROOM was simply redecorated
with no structural changes being
necessary.

14 I REVAMPED the main cloakroom
cupboard to maximize space.

15 THE DOWNSTAIRS cloakroom doubles as
the guest bathroom as it has a bath.

The Past Meets the Future

While a chic city home is often completely renovated at regular intervals, large country houses evolve over a different timescale. Not only is it very expensive to decorate huge rooms, but there is always something else to do, and if you tried to keep up with every changing fashion you would live permanently with the decorators. There's rarely the same need to make the most of every inch of space and light, and conservation issues may limit changes anyway. A room, therefore, may have to look good for twenty years. Even fifty years or more is not uncommon.

My client and her husband inherited this house as a young married couple with a limited budget and instantly understood the challenge they were faced with. Recognizing that the consequences of getting something wrong on this scale can be horrendous, they asked me to help.

LEFT: *Try gold or yellow to achieve light and grandeur simultaneously. I used my warm gold damask wallpaper for the entry hall, a guest's first introduction to the scale of this eighteenth-century house.*

A decorative scheme that will look good for decades

RIGHT: *Carpet is not practical over huge areas, but Oriental rugs can be replaced if they wear out in an area that receives heavy traffic, such as this inner corridor.*

THINK ABOUT FIRST IMPRESSIONS

The entry hall is the grand entrance to your house, even if you don't have something as dramatic and historic as this. It is where you can stamp your own personality or reflect the history of the house with a flourish. The entry hall is a well-used room – people walk through it every hour of every day – but nobody spends much time there, so you can be daring. Here there was the added challenge of its size and its heritage – my client felt that she was making a decorating decision to last until her young son grows up and takes over.

The starting point was not just the wonderful architecture of the house but the furniture already there, such as a pair of leather bucket chairs she had fallen in love with. Few people want to start completely from scratch and there are often real budgetary constraints, even in very grand homes. In this case, I felt that the decoration was like a picture frame – something that should enhance what was already there rather than fundamentally change anything.

When decorating an entry hall, remember that it has other rooms leading off it, so you need a colour that will go with many others. Here it also has a grand inner corridor adjacent to it. This entry hall has a large window, and I felt it was important to maintain the airy effect so that visitors are greeted with light as they enter. Yellows and golds are warm, sunny, versatile colours, so I decided on my gold damask wallpaper for this room. However, the inner corridor, which has almost no natural light, needed 'warming up', so for it I chose deep coral, which is warm, classic and gentle. An easy colour to live with, it will never look dated.

LEFT: *Echo patterns and textures throughout a room. In the hall, the stamped velvet of the curtains is similar to the damask wallpaper.* **ABOVE:** *The fireplace in the entry hall was original to the house, which gives a lovely, welcoming feel.*

Good lighting is crucial, and this is where you do need to be modern. Most historic houses were not built to have electric light, so don't feel that dreary pendant lighting is somehow traditional. Here we inset discreet halogen spotlights into the ceiling, to highlight the pictures and the glorious arches, and added traditional candlestick lamps on tables. The final effect is closer to the eighteenth-century original than the pendant lighting.

RIGHT: *It is better to devote a big chunk of your budget to one really outstanding piece. This oval mirror was one of our few purchases. The painting shows the house at harvest-time in Victorian days.*

ABOVE: *When converting antique china into lamps, never drill holes in it. For this lamp we inserted the light fixture with a stopper at the top and trailed the cord behind it.*
ABOVE RIGHT: *You can use a trimming to pull the colours in a room together.*

82

HOW TO TWEAK A CLASSIC

The sitting room had already been decorated in a lovely classic blue, but as I was doing the adjacent library, I was asked to 'tweak' the sitting room so that the two rooms flowed smoothly. I replaced some of the rugs, as rugs in adjoining rooms should work together. (A good tip when buying a rug, incidentally, is to look out for one that doesn't have a central motif, as it will be less restrictive when you are arranging furniture.) For extra seating I added a large stool, and some Edwardian chairs that I re-covered in pale blue. To stop the blue looking chilly, I reupholstered a sofa in coral and white. The stool is useful for coffee as well as seating, although you'd be surprised at how many people can crowd onto it when necessary.

For contrast, use flowers
as accent colours

LEFT: *Banish clutter when updating traditional style. This flower arrangement, portrait and pair of bonbonnières in the sitting room have a crisp simplicity.*
ABOVE: *Splashes of red prevent a blue room from looking cold – here I've echoed the colour of the jacket in the family portrait with red flowers.*

BELOW: *Painting everything – the walls, panelling, bookcases and fireplace – in the same shade creates a calm backdrop for a busy room.*
BELOW RIGHT: *Extra chairs in different styles stop a large room from looking like a furniture showroom.*

DECORATING A BUSY ROOM

The library is a grand room, but it is not precious. My clients have a young family and wanted a room where they could relax with furnishings that were resistant to the demands of children, although, of course, the architecture of the house also demands a certain level of elegance and style.

A rich toffee backdrop for calmness and warmth

When a room has plenty of space and light, high ceilings, lovely period features and good proportions, you might forget that you still need some kind of underlying discipline. What I have done here in the library is to ensure that the room has a calm base and a restricted palette of colours, so there can be a lot going on without it looking a mess.

LEFT: *Think about what kind of lighting each seating area needs. Every chair should have some kind of light. This lamp casts an ambient glow that warms up the entire room.* **RIGHT:** *On either side of the sofa are practical yet elegant swing-arm 'library lights' to provide good light for reading by.*

88

The bookcases in the library had been painted dark brown, which I wanted to lighten. Picking up on the lovely honey shades of old books, I painted everything – the walls, bookcases, panelling and fireplace – in the same rich toffee shade. This trick makes a busy room feel very calm.

A room of this size demands several seating areas, so plan these before buying furniture or dragging heavy pieces around. Write down what you intend to do in the room, whether it is watching television, reading, playing games or chatting to friends. Never skimp on this stage. If you have a television, for example, decide now where it will go – if its position is an afterthought, the seating may not be right. Take measurements and try out your plans with a scale drawing.

My brief was for the room to be used for reading, playing games and spending time with family and friends. There was already one window seat, so I added another to match it, making the perfect place for two people to play chess or board games. A corner of the room has become a reading area with two bucket chairs, a small table and a light. The rest of the seating – a deep red sofa, several comfortable armchairs, and a stool – is focused around the fireplace. Although the drawing room is the main entertaining area where guests congregate, any library or other sitting room benefits from having a range of seating: a sofa on which to sprawl and at least a couple of

Pull colours together with a pattern

ABOVE, CLOCKWISE FROM TOP LEFT: *Bill Amberg replaced the leather edging traditionally used to protect books from dust; cushions add pattern and interest; simple lamps minimise clutter in a busy room; the paisley pattern on two Edwardian chairs and some cushions contain all the colours in the room to pull the scheme together.*

BELOW: *A sofa with an upholstered back reduces the amount of work spent puffing up sofa cushions, and this sofa's deep red colour withstands grubby finger marks. Solid colours don't date as fast as patterns, and too much pattern can look busy, so use it on cushions rather than large expanses of upholstery.*

chairs that can be pulled into position at will. Different people like different heights of chair, too — something that should be borne in mind whatever your decorative style.

With so much furniture you need to be restrained not only in colour but also in design. We had some lovely crewel curtains made, and these are the only big areas of pattern in the room. The sofa and larger chairs are fairly plain, with pattern on cushions and smaller chairs.

LEFT: *Table flowers should be either high or low, so you can talk under or over them.*
ABOVE LEFT: *White china with a coat of arms is both grand and simple.*
ABOVE: *White linen napkins are classics.*
RIGHT: *Try two tables in a big dining room. To supplement the main table, I placed a smaller, round one, which can be laid for two or four, in a corner by the windows.*

92

My Challenge was the Panelling

This beautiful panelled dining room hadn't changed in a hundred years. Its panelling is fabulous but quite heavy, so the colour of the wall above it had to hold its own. A rich red is always a good choice – it is both strong enough to partner the panelling and classic enough for the future. The windows are large enough to take elaborate curtain treatments, but they are not the same as each other, so I opted for a plain, heavy chenille with French pleats. I added a tapestry border that echoes the design and colours of the carpet and topped it with a simple bullion-fringed pelmet. The treatment is grand enough for the scale of the room, but it's also simple enough to last and to work equally well for both windows.

1 This crewel fabric is a great vehicle for colour. Choose a good quality crewel, not a cheap one.

NINA'S NOTEBOOK

2 The leather trim on the bookcase was still in existence, but as it was in poor condition it was masterfully replaced by Bill Amberg.

7 This aqua blue flannel picks up the colour from the crewel curtains but is a more practical fabric than the crewel for the window seat.

6 Used on a pair of chairs and for cushions, this paisley echoes the colour scheme.

3 These fabrics were used on the sofa and chairs grouped around the fireplace at the other end of the library (see page 89).

KEY DECORATING DECISIONS

● This was a classically beautiful room to start with — gorgeous big windows, plenty of space and lots of lovely bookshelves. It's rare to start out with so few problems, and here I'd say that the main — probably the only — challenge was that a room filled with books absorbs light, so we had to pay careful attention to the lighting. Remember this particularly if you are decorating a room with a whole wall of books in it.

● In a room with lots of different seating areas — a games area, a reading corner, a place to chat — you need to go for variety and interest, so choose different ages and styles of chair and sofa.

4 This paisley chenille is a hard-wearing fabric for a much-loved chair. It seemed perfect for this corner and blends beautifully with the binding on the books and the leather trim.

5 A 'before' picture showing the library as it had been since the 1860s.

A BACHELOR PAD

We had to open out the layout of this 1930s apartment – which I worked on with the architect Eric Kohler – to make it a contemporary multi-purpose space, but my client, a single man, had some lovely furniture, so he wanted a masculine version of traditional style to go with it.

I believe in creating a sense of arrival – especially in a large, open-plan area. In the photograph on the left you can see where we brought the wall forward and added a pediment above the doorway, something you could try if you have high ceilings.

We defined the uses of different spaces in the entry hall/drawing room/dining area with wall colour and texture, a trick that can be used when decorating any large, multi-use room. One colour all over would have been overwhelming, but that doesn't mean you have to settle for white. For the front-door area I chose a warm golden yellow that echoes the curtain colour, while using red in the drawing room/dining area and a dark olive-green washable Alcantara suede on the stairway.

LEFT: *Include the odd mad touch like this marble umbrella stand from Keith Skeel. For the stair carpet I chose a Turkish carpet runner bordered in olive green.*

ABOVE: *This 'landmark' building already had marvellous architraves and stair detail, but you could consider replacing them in your own home.*
RIGHT: *Use patterns that contrast in scale.*

DECORATING ONE LARGE SPACE

It's always worth investing in good architectural details — here we cut back as much as possible the columns dividing the rooms. On the left of the photo above, you can see the added grandeur in the detail around the door of the understair cupboard. For sofas and chairs, choose colours that harmonize rather than match — I redid the chair in the foreground of the photo on the right in a wonderful gaufraged leather from an area in New York once famous for making gloves. The other chair is my Robert Browning chair, a very useful shape.

…cinnamon, red, olive green

LEFT: *When buying tie-backs, check the 'embrace' of the curtain, as some off-the-peg tie-backs aren't very long.*
ABOVE: *If you can't afford a complete set of fine china, just collect the pieces you need.*

The dining area leads out from the hall, so the table can be piled with books or laid for dinner. The glorious china came from a shop that I happened upon while wandering around New York looking for a coffee. I thought it was a real find — an antique shop crammed full of the most wonderful things — so imagine my surprise when I discovered that it was run by my friend Keith Skeel!

Opening up the room meant we had different shapes and sizes of windows. I harmonized them by using curtains and roman blinds (shades) in the same fabric as that of the sitting room — a useful approach when windows are different.

RIGHT: *The kitchen is an example of how to update: with new appliances and countertops you can have a brand-new look at a fraction of the cost.*
LEFT: *A detail of the kitchen door. This 1930s apartment has some wonderful patterns. Make the most of original features.*

REVITALIZING A KITCHEN

As you may have gathered, I'm a great believer in starting with what you already have and making the best of it – assuming it was well made in the first place – rather than ripping out everything and replacing it. A new kitchen is a huge expense, and this one was of good quality and in good condition, so all we had to do was spruce it up and modernize it with a few touches. Chic new appliances, especially large ones like refrigerators, are a great way of updating a look. Changing the countertops, rather than replacing all the cabinets, will personalize or modernize a kitchen at a relatively low cost.

We added a pot rack, replaced the countertop with slate and bought some great new appliances, such as the refrigerator and equipment for Chinese cooking. My client is a superb cook, so the shallow, glass-doored wall cupboard was invaluable for ingredients. Because the other cabinets were well positioned, we didn't change them. However, if you are refurbishing natural wood or painted cabinets, you should be prepared to re-sand and re-varnish – or repaint – them if they're looking tired. It will be only a fraction of the cost of replacement and will make all the difference.

104

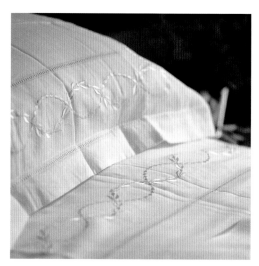

ABOVE, CLOCKWISE FROM LEFT: *The red detail in the fabrics echoes the wall colour; after a dinner party, redistribute table flowers around the house; exquisite linen adds delicacy.* **RIGHT:** *Try to fit some seating into a bedroom.*

MAKING THE MOST OF SPACE

These were two small rooms that we opened up into one long, thin room. Strong colour, like this red, works well to smooth out odd-shaped rooms, and adding a sitting area at one end makes the space work better. We lined one wall with storage, including bookcases and space for a television. Men usually don't like four-posters but the fine lines of this simple iron bedstead add a little grandeur without looking fussy.

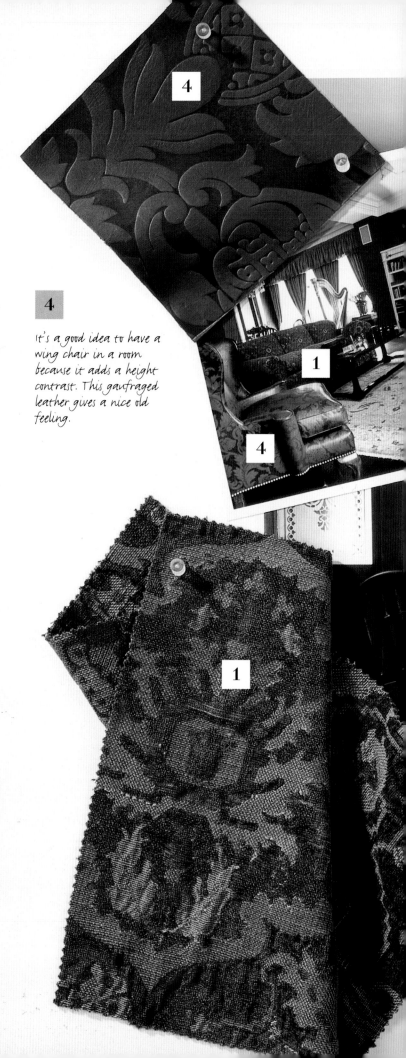

1 Use self-patterned fabrics on sofas and armchairs to make them look less large.

4 It's a good idea to have a wing chair in a room because it adds a height contrast. This gaufraged leather gives a nice old feeling.

NINA'S NOTEBOOK

KEY DECORATING DECISIONS

● This is in a beautiful landmark New York City apartment block, so our challenge was to bring together the building's own 1930s heritage and the owner's marvellous collection of eighteenth- and nineteenth-century English furniture, and unify it in a way that suits a modern lifestyle.

● Here the 'modern' element comes from the layout. One-room living offers the sense of space that we all need today. Once again, though, we knew it was important to open up this apartment without damaging or removing the heritage detail, such as the beautiful architraving, the wonderful stair banisters and balusters and all the other unique touches it had.

● When your furniture is stunning, you don't necessarily want to add a lot of pattern and colour as well. I like to use a controlled palette of colours, and here I've used gaufraged leather and self-patterned chenilles. They give texture and depth without setting themselves up as rivals to the lovely furniture and china. My spot silk, used on the dining chairs, is a nice nod to the 1930s architecture, and everything else relies on subtle shades and patterns.

1

2

3

2

When you are having
curtains made, be sure
they hang well. Lining
and interlining help
create a luxurious look.

3 Use furniture flexibly. This circular table is not just for
dinner parties – during the day it is piled with books and
flowers. If your dining table doubles as a 'hall' table, don't
leave too many chairs round it.

MODERN CLASSIC STYLE

Many people who love classic English style live in modern houses. Yet you can achieve the look if you take into account the strengths and weaknesses of the architecture. Modern houses and apartments often have wide, spacious rooms, large picture windows overlooking gardens and a free-flowing, flexible living floor that is partly or wholly open-plan.

However, they may also have odd-shaped rooms, awkward corners, or windows of different sizes and shapes in the same room. They have lower ceilings and, of course, the lack of architectural detail may make them seem bland.

This newly built apartment has both the good points and the design challenges of many modern houses, and, although we were starting from scratch, the brief was to create a natural and timeless look that could have evolved over many years.

If you want to give a modern home a traditional feel, draw upon the culture of where it is located. This was in Lebanon, so my starting point was the superb design and craftsmanship of this part of the world.

LEFT: *Reflect light wherever possible. Modern houses often have huge picture windows so we installed this large mirrored wall opposite one to reflect the daytime view. Candle sconces fitted onto the mirror make the room glitter at night.*

Use local colour and craftsmanship...

ABOVE LEFT AND RIGHT: *I loved scouring local antique shops for things that will help create a 'timeless' look. I often incorporate items clients already have, so this was a great treat.*
RIGHT: *Add character with architectural antiques – these stone columns were the starting point for much of the decorative detail. Also note the curtains: it's a good idea to avoid having a pelmet on low, wide windows and to keep the fabric harmonious with the walls.*

STARTING FROM SCRATCH

First get your planning right. Create smooth visual links from one room to the next. When rooms all flow into each other and can almost be opened up to make one huge space, it is vital to have a harmonious approach to colour and style. That doesn't mean every area must look the same — you can give each 'room' a strong visual identity of its own. Choose a basic palette of two — or, at the most three — harmonious colours. Aqua blues have a strong significance in this part of the world, as does gold. I chose the aqua and cream as I felt that it would draw on the Lebanon's heritage while being delightful to live with.

...to add character

112

ABOVE: *Rather than a painting, try panels or other decorative motifs. When my client bought two lovely mosaics, we had them inset.*

RIGHT AND FAR RIGHT: *If a country has a great history of design and craftsmanship, make the most of it. Inspired by the stone columns, we used local craftsmen to make radiator covers and other details.*

I often commission extra
architectural detail

I chose gold as the appropriate highlight for the aqua and cream theme. It's important not to get so locked into a colour scheme that nothing else can ever be brought into the room; always give yourself an escape route. In this apartment, it's provided by introducing red as a highlight in a series of specially commissioned rugs. These, once again, are similar but different, and could easily be moved from one room to the other to change the emphasis.

The other great challenge of many modern homes is a lack of architectural detail, but rather than adding a pastiche of inappropriate period elements, you can take one magnificent antique, work of art or architectural detail and use it as the inspiration for a theme throughout. Don't think of antiques as being just furniture, *objets* or paintings – here we incorporated four antique stone columns, creating a lovely contrast of old and new and the focus of my 'local' theme. My clients also bought two lovely mosaics, one of which was set into the floor as a 'rug' and the other as a wall panel in the central hall. They were also the inspiration for the newly carved stone fireplace, as well as for the design on the rugs.

114

RIGHT: *With the cultural history of Lebanon to draw on, I didn't want to settle for a standard French-style fireplace in the library. This was inspired and made locally.*
ABOVE: *A close-up of the wall frieze.*

HOW TO CREATE CHARACTER

A traditional classic home constantly evolves and it is the combination of old and new that gives it its character — the wealth of pattern and detail, the rich cornucopia of styles and the feeling of a heritage that has been built up over generations. Yet you can achieve the same effect in a few short weeks. Don't get everything from one shop or one kind of shop. Use art and antiques to create pattern and texture — for instance, it would have been quite wrong to clutter the library, pictured on the right, with

chintzes, much as I love them — because a trawl around your local antique shops will quickly yield something much more interesting. For example, I bought in London a superb collection of orientalist art, and while in Lebanon I bought a few smaller items, such as some attractive decanters, a collection of which I created overnight. We also bought some old Turkish panelling that didn't fit the available space exactly, and so we had it copied by local craftsmen, whose standard of workmanship was absolutely superb.

When you start with a modern building and a simple two-colour palette, it may initially all sound rather plain, and you may feel tempted to indulge in ornate curtains or furnishing fabrics. However, you will have a much more successful and flexible interior if you let your possessions, such as your art, collections and furniture, provide the detail and richness. Here, my clients have some wonderful Eastern antiques and both European and orientalist paintings, as well as pieces of both modern and antique furniture, and they all look good together because the backdrop is calm. If you do fall in love with an elaborate fabric, use it on cushions or on a small chair.

A theme for finishing touches pulls a home together

ABOVE: *This collection of antique decanters creates a lovely sense of history, as if acquired over generations. In fact, I bought them all from antique shops and markets, along with the ornamental box.*
ABOVE FAR LEFT AND LEFT: *Close-ups of the detail inspired by the stone columns.*

LEFT AND RIGHT: *The drawing room. Note how the accent colour in this soft, neutral scheme comes from the rugs. These are specially made Aubusson rugs with a Turkish motif, a nice way of drawing together European and Middle Eastern influences. Lamplight adds a key element to the classic look.*

I LIKE A CALM BACKGROUND

The drawing room is used regularly, both during the day and at night, which is why I have kept it calm and neutral. Walls and major pieces of furniture are all cream, and the colour comes from the rugs, paintings and artefacts. Not only is this a flexible background – it is easy to change things around at a moment's notice – but it would have been too much to have large blocks of strongly contrasting colour. A sofa is a good-sized piece of furniture, and many drawing rooms and sitting rooms have two or even more. Covering them in fabric that is at the opposite end of the colour spectrum from the walls – red sofas in a green room, for example, or blue sofas against orange walls – will usually jar the eye, so choose a colour that is similar to or

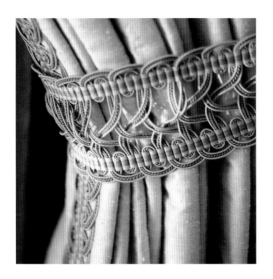

LEFT AND ABOVE: *Abstract patterns based on floral motifs are found in many details in this apartment, another theme that pulls it all together. The items come from all over the world: (clockwise from top left) English tie-backs, Irish mirror glass, Italian carving and Indian embroidery.*

harmonious with the walls, especially if your room is small. Seating needs to be agreeable physically as well as visually, so choose comfortable sofas and chairs – comfort is at the heart of my style.

The eclectic collection of art and artefacts in this room comes from Europe and the Middle East. This mixing of styles is, in fact, typical of classic English design, as exotic places and foreign travel have influenced English interiors since the days of the Grand Tour more than two centuries ago.

ABOVE: *Close-ups of the exquisite local embroidery. The women of Lebanon carried on this work throughout the war – it is really quite exceptional.*
RIGHT: *I chose an intense wall colour but minimized pattern so it doesn't look too busy.*

MY THOUGHTS ON DINING ROOMS

A dining room is where design rules can often be broken. For example, it's the only place where you can hang a chandelier in a low-ceilinged house, because if it hangs over the centre of the table it won't matter if it's low. When choosing one for this situation, go for something big and opulent – a small one will look half-hearted. If you need to move the tables around for different kinds of entertainment, ask your electrician to install an interrupter so it can easily be taken down.

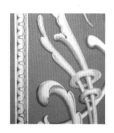

LEFT: *Mirrors add a dash of glamour, adding light and reflecting views. They also create a feeling of height.*
RIGHT: *Include imaginative combinations of china and glassware – they don't have to match. This china is by Christian Lacroix.*

125

A dining room needs some drama and glitter – you can use colour much more intensely. Here the blue from the rest of the apartment is executed in a sparkling, jewel-like aquamarine, and there are mirrors, candles, gilt and cut glass to dazzle and twinkle for a scintillating evening.

The chandelier and the candelabras also provide some contrasts of height – it's important not to fall into the trap of having absolutely everything low in a low room, as this would look bland. The lovely bucket chairs pictured on page 123 look good and work well here, but you could instead use high-backed dining chairs in this situation as another height contrast.

Dazzle with vibrant colour,
glass, gilt and mirrors

LEFT: *Mirrored furniture adds a dash of glamour, whether modern or traditional.*
RIGHT: *If you are going to use a pelmet in a low-ceilinged room, it should be neat, narrow and flush to the ceiling like this – the key is to keep it simple. A matching bed skirt, and a delicate scallop-edged bedcover add further softness. The lighting and flooring continue the themes seen elsewhere in the apartment.*

NOW I BREAK THE RULES...

In this bedroom there appear to be some contradictions of my advice on pages 63 and 118 about avoiding pelmets and fabric contrast in modern rooms with low ceilings, but it shows how the traditional English-bedroom look can be updated, simplified and adapted for a modern apartment. There are no four-posters, half-testers or elaborate curtain treatments here, but there is colour, fabric and detail – albeit in a restrained and tailored version.

I repeated here the apartment's basic colour theme – soft blues and creams – in yet another interpretation. These curtains, in a classic check, do not so much continue the wall colour as incorporate it, so a startling contrast is still avoided.

1 We commissioned these rugs specially and although they incorporate the cream and aqua of the colour scheme, I've added a bit of red as a wake-up call.

6 A frieze around the bookcases adds rich but subtle pattern.

5 A close-up of intricate detailing on a bookcase.

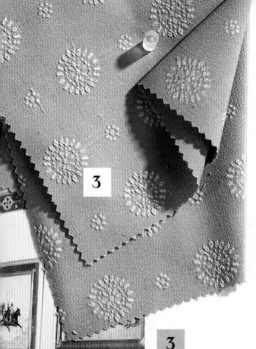

2

We had a wonderful time shopping for art and antiques for this apartment. There are no rules – pick what you love most and don't try to buy things simply because you think they might be a good investment.

3

I've kept pattern to a minimum on the fabrics – it gives you a very flexible background. This is the fabric used for the small chair near the fireplace.

4

The sofa fabric and its matching bullion fringe. There's a lot to be said for choosing fabrics and trimmings that are made to go together – at least someone else has done the hard work for you.

Nina's Notebook

Key Decorating Decisions

● Here we started from scratch, but wanted to establish a timeless, welcoming feel. We had to add architectural interest, character and a sense of place, so we drew on local traditions and craftsmanship, for which Lebanon is famous. If you move into a modern house in any part of the world, spend a little time looking at the traditions of the area – you don't have to turn your home into a pastiche, but local designs will probably look better than incorporating inappropriate French fireplaces or whatever is most fashionable at the time. Here, into what was hardly more than an empty shell, we added fireplaces, panelling, a frieze, mosaics and built-in bookcases.

● Spend money on getting the work done well. Architectural finish matters, and is much more noticeable than you think. Don't buy cheap plastic replicas from chain stores – get the real thing made. Here we had a fabulous culture to draw on, but wherever you live you can do your bit to keep local traditions alive.

● There is sometimes a temptation to paint a modern house or apartment all white, but you will get a more harmonious effect with a simple two- or three-colour palette. Once again, look to the heritage of your area – in this part of the world our theme colours of cream and aqua have real resonance, particularly when they are highlighted with gold.

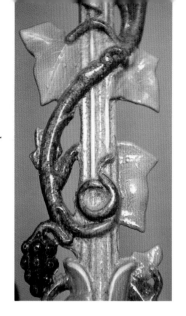

A HOUSE OF DISTINCTION

Here my brief was to help a stylish, modern family move into a classic town house. The former owners of the house had entertained a lot, so it was perfect for dinner parties, but not for family life.

The kitchen was the key. The family wanted to eat, do homework and entertain here, so we moved the kitchen into what had been the dining room. We had thought we would turn the old, smaller kitchen into a dining room, but decided to wait. It is now a fantastically useful back-up kitchen cum utility room. This is a good example of the importance of making changes only bit by bit if you're not quite sure what you want.

The other important factor was the marvellous period detail in the entrance hall. I don't often use white, but when you have something as dramatic and graphic as this, white looks clean, sharp and modern, and allows the beautiful classical features to speak for themselves.

LEFT: *This entrance hall doubles as a dining room for dinner parties. Modern brilliant white can soon look dead and grey, so choose an off-white paint shade. Here I used two and then painted the skirting boards (baseboards) black to echo the floor.*

Give furniture a new lease of life

LEFT: *Used for the curtains, the lovely red-and-gold fabric with a wide stripe looks as if it had been there for ever.*
RIGHT: *I used red velvet walls to mark out one end of the long drawing room as the cosy area, echoing the red in chairs and cushions at the other end.*

132

EVERYTHING IS RECYCLED

The family's former home had been a lovely country-rectory house and they wanted to bring some of that atmosphere with them. Although I often reuse clients' furniture, I think this project must be a recycling record, as my only new purchases were the crinkly gold-and-red curtains at this end of the drawing room. It's always such a joy to find the one fabric that pulls everything together – it might have been designed just for the purpose.

Recycling furniture doesn't mean you have to have the same colour theme in every house, as you can reupholster furniture, or create new colour combinations using existing fabrics. Here we re-covered all the chairs, the sofa and the stool, but the curtains on the main window were a deciding factor in the new colour scheme. The other element was the existing cornice and frieze, which we decided to keep. Taking these two elements, we came up with a palette of aqua, taupe and red. The end of the drawing room pictured on the right is the smaller, cosier, red end, while the other two thirds of the room is taupe. I didn't even buy new lamps, although I always believe in updating the look with new lampshades. Old shades get grubby, and buying new ones is a quick way of modernizing a scheme.

LEFT: *A view of the drawing room from the taupe end, looking through to the fireplace at the red end of the room.*
ABOVE: *The seating area at the taupe end of the drawing room.*

THE LONG VIEW

Use colour and furniture to divide a long room into different areas. Here there are three zones – an entrance area in the middle and seating areas at the ends – with columns and a large, square archway also delineating the spaces.

My clients have an extensive collection of pictures, so we decided to pack them together on the wall, country-house fashion. You can really only do this by trial and

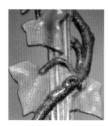

error, relying on your instinct, but I find it helpful to start with a big central picture – in this room, it was hung over the sofa. Plan the entire arrangement on the floor first. There aren't any rigid rules that you have to follow; just take a deep breath and make a start. Aim for a grouping that looks well balanced and pleasing to the eye, keeping the space tight between the frames. Different kinds of picture, such as oil paintings and watercolours, can look good together.

The curtains on the windows in the main drawing room came from my clients' last house. Though quite old, they were still beautiful, so we worked with the clients' own curtain-maker to cut out faded areas in the fabric and restyle the curtains. The swags from the previous curtains could not be reused, and so we opted for a flat pelmet with a pleat at the end of each window. We then added a gimp border to the edge of the curtains as the final touch.

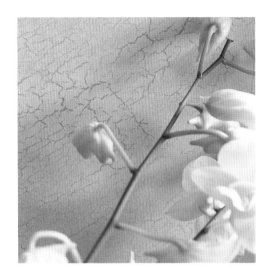

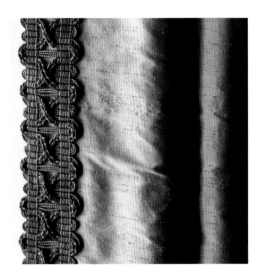

137

ABOVE: *Accessories really make a room, so if your home is looking a little tired, check fringes, braids and other details. Updating trimmings, replacing old frilly cushions with fashionable new ones and adding fresh flowers will wake the room up.*
LEFT: *A flat pelmet with pleats defining each window can look just as elegant as an elaborate swag and tail.*

Chuck out old-fashioned accessories

BELOW AND FAR RIGHT: *Blinds (shades) are better than curtains with banquette seating.* RIGHT: *Make something spectacular, like this painted and gilded cornice, your starting point. There are two plaster reliefs below the clock – a stylish variation on pictures.*

138

FROM FORMAL TO FAMILY

Although this was a generous-sized dining room, space was at a premium when it became a kitchen. Everybody in the family needed something different, whether it was an Aga range, somewhere to do homework or a plasma-screen TV.

We decided to retain the beautifully gilded cornice, making it the starting point for the colour scheme and setting it off with my Craquelure vinyl wallpaper.

The first thing you see when you come in is a bookcase, disguising the practical side of the kitchen from the hall. It's the end of a long central island unit with the sink in the middle and a back-up oven facing the Aga at the other end. The bay window holds a specially designed table and built-in banquette seating. The cushions create a comfortable back for the banquette, and they also help prevent draughts, while the evergreen box hedging, in window boxes outside, stops passers-by from looking in – a useful ploy when a window faces the street.

For windows behind banquette seating, blinds (shades) are better than curtains. Those used here are in my Aqua Manchu fabric, and the stripe on the banquette provides additional colour. I've kept everything neutral and natural, with surfaces in granite, teak and light wood. For the country feel that my clients missed from their last house, we placed a collection of pitchers and bowls on top of the cupboards.

1 With so many pictures, you need a strong or deep colo[ur] in the background. This taupe is a lovely rich neutra[l]

6 Beautifully done, the aqua frieze was one of the determining factors in the colour scheme. Prioritize carefully — however much you want to stamp your own mark on a house, don't assume you have to alter everything the previous owners did.

5 You can change a sofa fabric to any shade you like, so don't feel that your colour scheme has to be dictated by your current furniture.

4 My client already had this lovely rug, which, along with the frieze, dictated the colour scheme.

2

This gold fabric and bullion fringe were used for the pelmet (see page 136).

3

Don't have all your furniture the same height – a chair adds a different height to the room.

NINA'S NOTEBOOK

KEY DECORATING DECISIONS

● People often move up to a bigger house, or down to a smaller one, which means that they have to completely rethink their possessions. In this case the new house was much the same size as the old, and it was the atmosphere that was so different – the family moved from a country-house style rectory to a very smart town house.

● We wanted to keep some of the 'country' feeling of the old house, and achieved that with the great wall of pictures.

● There was no need to buy new furniture, just to re-cover and restore what we had. It is still not cheap – lots of people are surprised to find that restoring a good piece of old furniture can cost much the same as buying something brand new from a furniture store. You are rarely comparing like with like in terms of value, but it can still be significantly less than buying a really well-made new sofa. However, if your old sofa is a cheap one, don't bother – just start again.

● We used accessories and trimmings to update the look. Spend at least as much time looking for these as you do looking for bigger items.

● Rather than redo the existing aqua frieze, we based the colour scheme around it.

HOTEL AT HOME

Hotels used to be known for an anonymous, international kind of decorating that no one would have emulated at home, but now staying in a hotel can be the source of all kinds of design inspiration. Some people pick hotels for that reason alone. Good hotels have superb bedrooms and bathrooms, and there is an element of fantasy – such as in the boutique or hip hotels – which gives you a chance to spend some time in a particular design atmosphere before deciding to do something similar in your own home.

The Connaught Hotel is known as London's most gracious hotel, with a tradition going back many years, so I was delighted to be asked to renovate some of its bedrooms, along with the Connaught Bar, the Menu Restaurant and the Grill Room. The brief was to revitalize these rooms while retaining the Connaught's classic feel.

A modern twist to tradition

LEFT: *Updating a classic: the clean, modern lines of the sofa and chairs look good against the traditional panelling of the Connaught Bar. Note the small, high table – many people think tables used in front of sofas have to be long and low, but it's much easier to eat at something like this.*

LEFT: *Luxurious materials are often practical. This mohair and lizardskin fabric won't show finger marks.*
RIGHT: *The Connaught Bar. Throughout the downstairs rooms at the Connaught I used chairs I had re-covered in similar fabrics so that they could be taken from room to room when necessary.*

A flexible layout

144

ALWAYS LIST THE PRIORITIES

My first task was to breathe life into a rather disused room now known as the Connaught Bar, which had turned into a sitting room in which no one sat. Like houses, even good hotels have their 'lost' corners, and it was a priority to make this room feel welcoming. The result is shown on the right and on page 142.

My two favourite principles came into play here. The first is to get the space working properly before decorating, which meant looking at how people flowed through the room. In this case, they didn't. Once in, there was no way out, or at least that's how it felt. I added a second door, so that people could come in, have a drink, and then go on through to the restaurant. Thus it became more central to the regular comings and goings of the hotel.

I also believe that if you have beautiful features you should make the most of them rather than change everything. The lovely panelling looked dingy, so I enriched it here in the bar by painting it a creamy toffee colour and in the Menu Resturant on the following pages we retained the mahogany. As it had become rather 'orange' over the years, we renovated it to make it richer. Above the panelling, instead of white which can look flat and dirty, I used rich, warm colours, such as a paler toffee and olive green in the Menu Restaurant, lacquering it for extra depth.

Warm colours and simplified style

The Menu Restaurant is the most traditional of the three rooms, with dark panelling and thick curtains. I was asked to retain this atmosphere but add some contemporary touches.

You can always update a room and improve the atmosphere with good lighting. I had library lights made for this room, and also ran a discreet line of lighting within the panelling so that it glows upwards. This is a trick you could use at home with bookcases. In the Connaught Bar I hung huge pendant bowls from Denton in front of the mirrors. They seem to go on and on – a good example of the value of thinking about mirrors when you're planning lighting.

Window treatments are another update area. If you have lovely panelling, elaborate curtains may be over-egging the pudding. Here, I decided on neat, modern blinds (shades) – in spot silk to match the lacquered wall above the panelling.

Behind the panelling we discovered two old fireplaces which I decided to have reopened to create two separate focal points for the room. I chose a classic bolection moulding and had it made in bronze to give it a more contemporary twist. The fireplace is also lined in the bronze, and the line of gas firelight dancing across the interior when it is lit gives a warm glow. People are tempted to eliminate the hearth but I always think this looks wrong. However, if you are very short of space and it is only a gas fire, you can make your hearth less deep than is required for a real fireplace.

LEFT: *Hang pictures on panelling as you would on plain walls.*
OVERLEAF: *The Menu Restaurant – note how the fireplace creates a focal point without intruding into the room.*

LEFT AND BELOW: *If you want more colour, control pattern carefully. Here, the three-colour palette looks cool and modern because we've used texture instead of pattern. The one dramatic flourish is a flower painting by Patrice Lombardi.*

151

My brief in the Grill Room was to keep the look light and fresh, with the highest attention to quality and detail. This is the most contemporary of the three rooms, with a theme of cream, olive green and aubergine (eggplant). The green walls have a lightly textured waxed finish, which gives a little more depth and luminosity to an otherwise plain wall. There is a lot of ornamental plasterwork such as cornicing in this room, much of which had been gilded. However, this would look unnecessarily fussy when a light, modern feel is required. Instead of gilding, therefore, I've taken the same green paint colour over it all, which makes the room feel more serene.

This is a room where texture takes the place of pattern – a nice, relaxed, modern concept. The chairs are the same as those in the Menu Restaurant, because furniture is much more flexible if you can move it from room to room. At home you can have extra dining chairs in a sitting room, dining room and drawing room. If they are similar patterns they can be interchanged when necessary.

The curtains, once again, are plain, but have texture in the detail: a pretty glass-bead edging. And because the view is an unexciting courtyard, I have used bamboo blinds at the window which filter the light beautifully.

ABOVE LEFT AND ABOVE: *Occasional tables are invaluable in bedrooms if they are big enough for everything you want to have on them.*
RIGHT: *When refurbishing a bedroom, splash out on luxurious new bedlinen, and add a throw.*

152

BORROWING FROM HOTEL BEDROOMS

A hotel bedroom, like a guest room in the home, has to appeal to a wide range of people, and these rooms were previously quite chintzy. I love chintz in the right place, but if a room is slept in by businessmen, young couples and a wide variety of single people, floral patterns are too feminine and homey. I decided on a striped wallpaper, a pattern both traditional and modern, and which appeals to men as well as women. The bedroom pictured on the right is red because it is one of the smaller rooms, and red has a grandeur that makes it seem more important than it is. A yellow stripe is particularly good in the larger, lighter rooms.

The Connaught has lovely furniture and because of that there was no question of buying anything new. However, the rooms were overcrowded, so simply removing several pieces freshened them up. Most bedrooms need this kind of tweaking from time to time – even if you haven't the time or budget for a proper refurbishment, make sure you reassess the pictures and furniture, usually removing rather than adding to what you already have. Here I regrouped pictures and simplified them, which created a calmer effect.

The hotel has bought new, larger double beds, something that even quite small rooms can accommodate if clutter is kept to a minimum.

1 Modern and practical, textural fabric doesn't show wear as much as plain fabric does and so is ideal for chairs.

2 The texture of the fabric is echoed by that of the bamboo blind.

6 This waxed paint effect replaced the previous green-and-gold paintwork, keeping the colour but modernizing the effect.

5 For practicality, choose a self-patterned carpet.

a Campbell 2002 — The Grill Room

The clear Perspex (Plexiglas) pole and the French-headed curtains give a contemporary look.

One striking piece of art really makes a difference. Think big. Be dramatic. Many art galleries will now let you try works out in your own home — do ask.

NINA'S NOTEBOOK

KEY DECORATING DECISIONS

● The Grill Room at the Connaught shows how you can have a calm, relaxing, stylish atmosphere in what is actually a busy and well-frequented room. We wanted it to feel like the most contemporary of the Connaught restaurants. When you have a beautiful, historic room to start with – this has lots of lovely period detail and high ceilings – you have to achieve a harmonious balance between old and new rather than ripping everything out and adding lots of modern furniture. The aim was crisp and contemporary, not hard and modern.

● Contemporary, in the context of a period house, means respecting period detail and treating it simply, then keeping fabrics, artwork and other detail harmonious and unfussy. Thankfully the days are long gone when 'modernizing' a house meant ripping out its fireplaces and cornicing.

● Modern doesn't have to mean using white paint everywhere. In the wrong context white can look flat and sad. This dining room was traditionally green so I decided to use a subtle, contemporary shade of green, with aubergine and cream.

● This project offers one of the best lessons on practicality that I can think of. A restaurant has to look elegant, luxurious and welcoming day after day – and it must be very hard-wearing. It is subjected to far greater wear than the average family dining room, and whatever happens during the day, it has to reopen its doors the following morning looking as stylish and sparkling as ever. This means that the decorating decisions made in a restaurant do have to be very practical indeed, however luxurious the end result.

CLASSIC REFRESHMENT

This gentlemen's club in the United States, which was modelled on English clubs, is in a beautiful old building with wonderful collections of art and artefacts. Here the brief was to update it without losing its character, adding a warmth and zing that would appeal to younger members.

Once again, I started with the entry hall, for which I chose my Wolsey trompe l'oeil panelled wallpaper. A curved wall is difficult to decorate with pictures, and so wallpaper comes into its own. As in many halls, the stairs are the major feature, therefore a good stair carpet is important. This olive-green carpet from Braquenie et Cie picks up on the tones of the marble floor.

FAR LEFT AND LEFT: *Carpet runners held in place by brass or steel rods and showing off the wood at the edges give a more classic look than fitted stair carpet taken to the edges. Avoid too distinctive a border design for a circular staircase, as one side will have to be cut more than the other, affecting the pattern.*

Use a mirror
to reflect fine features

LEFT: *Silver from the club's collection.*
ABOVE: *Period detail on the stair banister.*
RIGHT: *Use a mirror to frame the reflection of something beautiful, like the curved stairway.*

CONTINUE THE THEME UPSTAIRS

Upstairs, the old-fashioned elevator and the stairs meet in a beautiful high-ceilinged space. I continued the wallpaper up to this floor — it's always a good idea to carry a theme upstairs to avoid any awkward breaks. In a space like this, wallpaper works better than paint because the pattern — even a discreet, self-coloured one like this — breaks up the vast expanses of wall.

The mirror was owned by the club and was perfect for this position, reflecting the curved staircase. The principle, however, works for any house — if you have something lovely, reflect it in a mirror, even a plain one.

PANELLING ESSENTIALS

The bar is a wonderful panelled room where pictures and collections can be displayed and members can retreat for a quiet game of backgammon or cards. People often forget that panelling, like any other surface, wears out after years of exposure to light, heat and dirt; the colour of the wood fades and distorts and the varnish wears thin. It is a big investment to strip, polish and re-varnish a panelled room, but consider how often you redecorate ordinary walls. Panelling doesn't have to be done as often as unpanelled walls, but treatment is occasionally necessary. Therefore, restoring the richness and life to the wood was my starting point.

Leather epitomizes the gentlemen's club, but it doesn't have to be black or brown. Having yet more brown on the leather banquette seating would have looked dull, so I chose a deep greeny-black shade, which adds depth, warmth and interest.

The lighting came next. To keep this room cosy we used standard lamps and picture lights only, and I had the lampshades made out of marbled paper. People used to have lampshades made – or would make them themselves – as a matter of course, but now they buy them in shops. Nevertheless, personally commissioning something is a good way of getting exactly what you want. Standard lamps have slightly fallen from fashion over the years, but these elegant, classical stands would look good in any setting, from traditional rooms to somewhere quite modern. They keep the effect uncluttered because they don't need side tables, and they offer a good, high-up task light if you want to read or play games.

The club has a variety of splendid collections, not just of pictures but of all kinds of things, like the pewter plates pictured on the left. One of the greatest pleasures in any refurbishment is to take a long, hard look at everything you have and work out new ways of displaying it to better advantage. This is also a good opportunity to do any repairs, cleaning and restoration that are needed, as your possessions may otherwise languish for years without attention.

161

I loved turning this club into

a real home

WHEN CONTRAST WORKS

From the cosy embrace of the bar, with its muted lighting, leather and dark panelling, you step into the glittering atmosphere of the dining room. Here we were particularly lucky, because the club already had a beautiful dining table and exquisite collections of silver, paintings and furniture.

I frequently advise people to maintain one colour or theme throughout a floor or even an entire home, or to ensure that colours seen through doors to different rooms harmonize with or lead into each other. That is particularly good advice for small spaces, but this is not a small space – here, dramatic contrast is the keynote. I decided that it would be effective to walk from the dark to the light, and if you are decorating a large home you can do the same, especially when you move from an everyday room to one that is special. We therefore painted the walls a deep cream.

I also did something rather brave – I blocked out two windows flanking the fireplace and replaced them with huge mirrors. Sometimes mirrors create as much light as windows do, particularly in a room that is used mainly at night. Another factor was that the view and light on that side had been blanked out by newer buildings. If there are regulations affecting the outside of your house, or if the windows really affect the appearance of the exterior, you can't do it; otherwise, give windows that don't let in much light a long, hard look and ask yourself whether that space could be used better if you blocked them up.

Lighting is probably the most important aspect of decorating a dining room. It should be subtle yet sparkling. Bright overhead lights, other than chandeliers, are inappropriate at dinner. Even chandeliers should be fitted with dimmer switches, and you should spend some time experimenting with the level of brightness. If it's too dark no one can see their food, but if it's too light the atmosphere will be spoiled and people's complexions will look drained. Wall lights are a good option for dining rooms, and by having light sconces fitted to the huge mirrors in this room I was able

163

ABOVE: *To avoid harsh overhead lighting in a dining room, set wall-light sconces into a mirror. Picture lighting adds another level of subtle ambient light, as do the candelabras down the centre of the table.*

to achieve a dazzling reflected effect. They need to be installed by an expert, but it's not difficult. Choose mirrors that are fairly simple and let the wall sconces do the glittering. Not every room is suited to a chandelier, and a similar effect can be achieved with ornate table candelabras. With the picture lights and mirror lights, that was all the lighting this room needed.

RIGHT: *When using a strong colour like red, reduce the intensity by painting the dado (wainscot) white or cream. This red is lacquered for extra depth.*

A CLUB ATMOSPHERE

T his is the heart of the club – a large, cosseting room with leather chairs and tall, swagged windows. When people think about clubs, they think of leather chairs, and this is no exception. The club was keen to keep these, but I believe that it's also important to have a selection of different styles and shapes of chair in any comfortable drawing room. People prefer chairs that are lower or higher, softer or harder, according to their height, physical characteristics and personal preferences. At any rate, a chair for reading is not necessarily the chair you are most relaxed in when having a discreet conversation.

It's also useful to have a mix of lighter and heavier chairs and sofas. Sofas are generally fixed pieces, but the lighter leather chairs can more easily be pulled up to

Left and below: In this window treatment the lining – visible in the gracefully hanging tails (cascades) – matches the walls, and the fringing harmonizes with the main fabric. Buy tassels, trimmings and tie-backs from the same range as the fabric to ensure they will look right together.

a grouping, or drawn aside for a private read. Here there is a wide range of seating, from sofas and chairs to a bench and a padded fender around the fire. Whether you're furnishing a gentlemen's club or your own drawing room, think about all these considerations and build in flexibility as well as comfort.

Tall, stately windows demand grand curtain treatments, but budgets are a real consideration when such large amounts of fabric are involved. Top-of-the-range fabric isn't essential, but you do need to know whether it will hang well, so consult a curtain-maker or the fabric shop. It's particularly important if you want to have lavish swagged pelmets like these, as not every fabric is suitable for such treatment. The way a fabric hangs is as important as its colour or pattern.

Pattern is a major consideration in a big room. Too much pattern would have looked overblown on these curtains, so we picked a calm fabric and added interest with the shape, the lining and the fringing. The result is grand without being overwhelming or fussy. There is a mixture of patterns on the sofas and chairs – some are small and neat, while one or two sofas have larger patterns, but all the colours harmonize. You will achieve a more successful effect if your walls, sofas, floor treatment and curtains don't all shout at each other. Keep contrasting colours for smaller chairs, cushions and accents such as flowers.

168

ABOVE LEFT: *Embellish a plain curtain with a braid or border.*
LEFT: *A few tulip heads floated in a glass bowl.*
RIGHT: *Carry a colour theme through in the detail – in the drawing room, the red from elsewhere is echoed on the small chairs and the cushion fringing.*

FLEXIBLE AND WELCOMING

For the ladies' drawing room, I was asked to create a comfortable, pretty room, and I chose another of my favourite decorating colours, yellow, because it is so cheerful. Also, it looks good with splashes of red, thus connecting it with the rest of the house.

If you're furnishing a large room, then back-to-back sofas can create two seating areas, but you shouldn't necessarily buy them as one piece: it is sometimes better to have two separate sofas so that you can move them for a party. Follow the theme of double-facing furniture to keep the look uncluttered – the long, thin table serves both sofas. The central standard lamps are also worth copying – but remember to have sockets (outlets) wired into the floor, to avoid trailing cords.

Make a single bedroom feel truly grand

LEFT: *An old-fashioned four-poster, too small to be a double bed, can make a single room look dramatic and elegant. When furnishing with a four-poster, you will need higher bedside tables.*
RIGHT: *I matched the trim on the bed's tailored pelmet to the cord on the walls.*

SMARTEN UP A SMALL BEDROOM

As this is a gentlemen's club, only men stay here – wives and girlfriends are not allowed – so the bedrooms I decorated are single rooms. The bedroom pictured here is a good example of how special a single room can be. Far from being a sad box room, it can feel like the best bedroom in the house.

You can put a small four-poster in a little room, whether the ceilings are high or low – it will make the room feel grand. Often an antique bed is only four feet wide, which was a double bed in the days when people were much smaller, but it would hardly qualify as such now. For a single room, however, it is an ideal choice.

With its straight pelmet and valance, the American style of dressing a four-poster, as shown on the left, is more tailored than the gathered English style. The pagoda-style canopy on this bed made it an ideal candidate for a streamlined approach, which would show off the canopy's lovely lines, and I picked up on the Chinese feel with my Asticou fabric. As the bedroom is a man's room, I used this teal-green colour.

I echoed the smart tailored look with a self-striped wallpaper in two shades of off-white, outlined with a cord that matches the four-poster pelmet. All these lines create quite a graphic effect – appropriately masculine but still luxurious.

1 Find one fabric that you love and make that your central point. Choose all the other fabrics to go with it – and have faith in your first choice. You may, in the end, decide to use it only on something small – but it's still your 'anchor'.

2 Think about what the room will look like from the door when you first enter and are n yet aware of much detail. You need some immediate dramatic impact, and here it's achieved with the swagged curtains.

7 We reused the existing red leather dining chairs.

obscured a view of
conditioning units
h a cream linen
nan blind (shade)
ich still lets in some
ht. It looks much
arter and more
temporary than nets.

4

The dining room
before redecoration

4

2

3

6

NINA'S NOTEBOOK

KEY DECORATING DECISIONS

● This is the club dining room where I blocked up a pair of windows flanking the fireplace. It may seem sacrilege to do something like this, because light is so important, but it's really worth thinking about what windows are achieving and what they look out onto. In this case they were obscured by another building, which had been constructed later, and was now blocking out the original light and view.

● Unless there are aesthetic reasons or restrictions concerning changes to the exterior of your house, you could consider changing the windows or the doors. If you've engaged an architect, I'd urge you to discuss whether you can make these elements work better for you. You can turn windows into doors or doors into windows, block them up, enlarge them or re-site them. However, it's not a do-it-yourself job, as there may be regulations to follow or structural issues, and the final finish is extremely important.

● I installed big mirrors on either side of the fireplace with lights fixed onto them. This is another job that must be meticulously planned, but the end result is a lovely twinkle. I'd certainly suggest considering it as an alternative to the more usual position of the mirror, over the fireplace.

6

On the left is a 'before' picture
of the windows I blocked up and,
beside it, a close-up of the
mirror glass that replaced it. I
love distressed old mirrors – they
are less harsh than modern ones.

5

A really rich rug will create
a great atmosphere and is
more forgiving in a dining
room than carpet.

SUPPLIERS

HOME COLLECTION

Nina Campbell Ltd
9 Walton Street,
London, SW3 2JD
Tel: +44 (0) 20 7225 1011
www.ninacampbell.com

FABRICS & WALLPAPERS

UK
Osborne & Little
304 King's Road,
London, SW3 5UH
Tel: +44 (0) 20 7352 1456

USA
ATLANTA
Grizzel & Mann
351 Peachtrees Hills Avenue,
Suite 120, Atlanta, GA 30305
Tel: +1 404 261 5932

BOSTON
Osbourne & Little, Inc
One Design Centre Place,
Suite 551, Boston, MA 02210
Tel: +1 617 737 2927

CHICAGO
Osborne & Little, Inc
Merchandise Mart, Suite 610,
Chicago, IL 60654
Tel: +1 312 467 0913

CLEVELAND
Gregory Alonso, Inc
Ohio Design Center,
23533 Mercantile Road,
Suite 113, Beachwood,
OH 44122
Tel: +1 216 765 1810

DALLAS
ID Collection
1025 N. Stemmons Freeway,
Suite 745, Dallas TX 75207
Tel: +1 214 698 0226

DANIA BEACH
Ammon Hickson, Inc
1855 Griffin Road, Suite B364
Dania Beach, FL 33004
Tel: +1 954 925 1555

DENVER
Shanahan Collection
Denver Design Center,
595 S. Broadway, Suite 100-S,
Denver, CO 80209
Tel: +1 303 778 7088

HONOLULU
International Design
Sources, Inc.
560 N. Nimitz Highway,
Suite 201E, Honolulu,
HI 96817, Hawaii
Tel: +1 808 523 8000

HOUSTON
I D Collection
5120 Woodway, Suite 4001,
Houston, TX 77056
Tel: +1 713 623 2344

KANSAS CITY
Designers Only
5225 W. 75th Street,
Prairie Village, KS 66208
Tel: +1 913 649 3778

LAGUNA NIGUEL
Blake House Associates
Laguna Design Center,
23811 Aliso Creek Road,
Suite 171, Laguna Niguel,
CA 92677
Tel: +1 949 831 8292

LOS ANGELES
Osborne & Little, Inc
Pacific Design Center,
8687 Melrose Avenue, Suite
B643, Los Angeles, CA 90069
Tel: +1 310 659 7667

MINNEAPOLIS
Scherping Westphal, LLC
International Market Square,
275 Market Street, Suite 209,
Minneapolis, MN 55405
Tel: +1 612 822 2700

NEW YORK
Osborne & Little, Inc
979 Third Avenue, Suite 520,
New York, NY 10022
Tel: +1 212 751 3333

PHILADELPHIA
JW Showroom, Inc
The Marketplace,
2400 Market Street, Suite 304,
Philadelphia, PA 19103
Tel: +1 215 561 2270

ST. LOUIS
Design & Detail
2731 Sutton Boulevard,
Suite 100, Maplewood,
MO 63143
Tel: +1 314 781 3336

SAN FRANCISCO
Osborne & Little, Inc
101 Henry Adams Street,
Suite 435, San Francisco,
CA 94103
Tel: +1 415 255 8987

SCOTTSDALE
Dean-Warren
Arizona Design Center,
7350 N. Dobson Road,
Suite 135, Scottsdale, AZ 85256
Tel: +1 480 990 9233

SEATTLE
Joan Lockwood Collection
5701 6th Avenue S., Suite 203,
Seattle, WA 98108
Tel: +1 206 763 1912

STAMFORD
Osborne & Little, Inc
90 Commerce Road, Stamford,
CT 06902
Tel: +1 203 359 1500

WASHINGTON DC
Osborne & Little, Inc
300 D Street SW, Suite 435,
Washington, DC 20024
Tel: +1 (202) 554-8800

CANADA
Primavera
160 Pears Avenue, Suite 110,
Toronto, Ontario M5R 3P8
Tel: +1 416 921 3334

EUROPE
AUSTRIA
Osborne & Little Ltd
Tel: +43 1 79 56 74 56

BELGIUM & LUXEMBOURG
Osborne & Little Ltd
Tel: +32 200 6349

CROATIA
Meblo Trade, Zagreb
Tel +385 1 6596 412

CYPRUS
Charilaos Stavrakis Ltd
27-29 Griva Dighenis Avenue,
PO Box 1919, Nicosia
Tel: +357 2 763 964

CZECH REPUBLIC
Paráda
Na Zlíchnove 288,
150 00 Praha 5
Tel:/Fax: +420 2 51 55 47 70

DENMARK
Form 4 Aps, Søborg
Tel + 45 2989 2639

FINLAND
OY S W Lauritzon & Co AB
Teerisuonkuja 6,
00770 Helsinki
Tel: +358 9 777 1800

FRANCE
Osborne & Little Ltd.
Tel: +33 1 55 69 81 06

GERMANY
Osborne & Little Ltd.
Tel: +49 69 50 98 51 71

GIBRALTAR
Denville Designs
62 Engineer Lane
Tel: +350 74 4012

GREECE
Ottimo Ltd Com. Centre 2
Agora
10-12 Kifisias Avenue,
Athens 15125
Tel: +30 210 684 8107

HOLLAND
Wilhelmine van Aerssen
Agenturen
Hoogte Kadijk 143 F2-3,
1018 BH Amsterdam
Tel: +31 20 640 5060

HUNGARY
Dekor Classic KFT
Üzlet: 1074, Budapest DOB U.6
Tel:/Fax: +361 342 2720

ITALY
Donati Remo & CSpA
Corso Tassoni 66,
10144 Torino
Tel: +39 011 437 6666

MALTA
Camilleri Paris Mode
Annunciation Square,
Sliema SLM06
Tel: +356 21 344 838

NORWAY
Poesi Interiøragentur AS
Erling Skjalgssonsgt 19a,
0267 Oslo
Tel: +47 22 12 81 80

POLAND
Decodore, Warsaw
Tel +48 22 648 9320

PORTUGAL
Pedroso e Osorio
Rua Fernando Lopes 409/2,
4150-318 Porto
Tel: +351 22 616 5030

SLOVAKIA
Décor Interior
Belopotochého 1,
811 05 Bratislava
Tel/Fax: +421 2 5443 5262

SPAIN
Gaston y Daniela
Hermosilla 26, 28001 Madrid
Tel: +34 91 485 2590

SWEDEN
Cadoro Agenturer AB
Nybrogatan 77,
114 40 Stockholm
Tel: +46 8 660 2346

SWITZERLAND
French Speaking: Quid Novi
Tel: +044 511 80 13
German Speaking: BBD
Tel: +044 511 80 13

TURKEY
Felko AS
Abdi Ipekci Cad, Isparta Palas
No.19/2, Nisantasi, Istanbul
Tel: +90 212 234 2435

WORLDWIDE
ARGENTINA
Miranda Green, Buenos Aires
Tel: +54 11 4802 0850

AUSTRALIA
Mokum Textiles (Pty) Ltd,
NSW Tel: +61 2 9380 6188

BERMUDA
Howe Enterprising, Hamilton
Tel: +1 441 292 1433
Hamma Enterprises Ltd,
Hamilton
Tel: +1 441 292 8500

BRAZIL
Miranda Green Do Brazil,
São Paulo
Tel: +55 11 280 0448

CHILE
La Canel, Santiago
Tel +2 7915 327

COLOMBIA
Denise Webb Diseño Interiors,
Bogota
Tel: +57 12 556 194

EGYPT
The Design Emporium, Cairo
Tel: +202 348 3848

HONG KONG
Altfield Enterprises Ltd,
Hong Kong
Tel: +852 2524 3318

INDONESIA
PT International,
Jakarta, Selatan
Tel: +62 21 719 7308

ISRAEL
Schecther, Tel Aviv,
Tel +97 2 36815655

JAPAN
Manas Trading, Inc, Tokyo
Tel: +81 3 5322 6478

KENYA
Caroline Fox, Nairobi
Tel: +254 20 376 5095

KOREA
SEDEC Ltd, Seoul
Tel: +82 2 549 6701

LEBANON
Belbol Ameublement s.a.r.l,
Beyrouth
Tel: + 961 1 563 658

MALAYSIA
Janine Sdn Bhd, Kuala Lumpur
Tel: +60 3 2148 2840

MEXICO
Attelage Representaciones
Textiles, Naucalpan de Juárez
Tel: + 52 55 3536 3858

**MIDDLE EAST (Agent for
IRAN, JORDAN, KUWAIT,
LEBANON, OMAN, QATAR,
SAUDI ARABIA, SYRIA,
UNITED ARAB EMIRATES)**
Casana LLC
Smark Building, Office No 8,
Sheikh Zayed Rd, Dubai,
United Arab Emirates
Tel +971 4339 58 39

MOROCCO
Rodesma Textiles Deco,
Casablanca
Tel: +212 2229 7294

NEW ZEALAND
Mokum Textiles Ltd,
Auckland
Tel: +64 9 379 3041

PERU
Romantex SA, Lima
Tel: +511 441 3339

SINGAPORE
Just the Place, Singapore
Tel: +65 6735 3389

SOUTH AFRICA
Home Fabrics, Johannesburg
Tel: +27 11 265 9000

TAIWAN
Solari Design, Taipei
Tel: +886 2 2327 9558

THAILAND
Charoen International
Tel: +66 2712-2552-6

UAE
AATI Decoration, Abu Dhabi
Tel: +971 2 3780 101

**WORKS BY SOPHIE
CORYNDON**

Lucy B. Campbell Fine Art
123 Kensington Church Street,
London W8 7LP
Tel: +44 (020) 7727 2205

INDEX